MW00935774

Modern Zanzibar Cuisine

For my mom, Faye Healy, a wise and intellectual lady who always help me to stay on the right path and to build an outstanding future. You are the person who gives me courage and integrity to stand for what is best in my life. You are and always be my best and lovely mom!

Your loving son,
Yassir

Modern Zanzibar Cuisine

Benn Haidari

ATHENA PRESS
LONDON

Modern Zanzibar Cuisine
Copyright © Benn Haidari 2006

All Rights Reserved

ISBN 1 84401 595 5

First Published 2006 by
ATHENA PRESS
Queen's House, 2 Holly Road
Twickenham TW1 4EG
United Kingdom

Printed and bound by Antony Rowe Ltd., Eastbourne

Author's Note

Benn Haidari

There is something fascinating and moving about the historic recipes of Zanzibar and Pemba islands. They are an intimate link with the past, revealing the sensuous quality, the spicy tastes and smells and feel of culinary culture gone by. And they also tell us much about the past. This book contains Zanzibari, Pemban and Comorian recipes from various sources dating back as far as the tenth century AD. I tried to bring some insight into medieval Zanzibar through recipes of the time, and to illuminate the development of Zanzibari cuisine and my own modern dishes against a historical and sociological background.

The publication of the book, which will be a resource of great importance to Zanzibari chefs, is especially exciting for me because it is the culmination of a major enterprise which stretches all the way back to a suggestion I made some fifteen years ago to my former wife. In 1989 I was making films on food and cookery from different countries around the world, including Zanzibar. It struck me then that it was a great pity I could not continue with these films, which were essential viewing for many Finns in those days; they were beginning to travel not only to European countries but also to African countries, and were therefore happy to watch these partly documentary and partly comedy films. Fifteen years may seem like a long time to wait, but the original idea has grown substantially in the interim…

The Spice Islands, before the revolution of 1964, enjoyed the Golden Age of a civilisation at its most glorious. The civilisation was more advanced and sophisticated than any European civilisation at the time, and the food – at least that of the upper classes – was immensely rich and refined. To contemporary palates, Zanzibari dishes are far tastier than European ones, and they relate to Middle Eastern and Asian dishes today in a way that European ones cannot. You can recognise in these recipes the roots of dishes from Iran and India, Turkey, North Africa and elsewhere in the Middle East.

When I began researching Zanzibari dishes in the late 1989, there were some Zanzibari cookery books written in the Swahili language. When I asked the librarian at the Finnish Library to help me to find something on Zanzibari cooking, he could not produce any book containing modern or ancient Zanzibari cookery in English; but there was a lot of material relating to medieval Arabian gastronomy.

My excitement was partly due to a feeling of familiarity. I had been collecting Zanzibari recipes from people for several years and many of the older ones rang a bell. There were similar words, similar combinations of ingredients and flavourings, and similar descriptions of techniques to those I had already heard of. It was thrilling to trace the origins of dishes such as *Ndizi na utumbo* (Bananas with calf intestines), and recipes done by my own family at home. For months and months I cooked these Zanzibari dishes and entertained friends, including Europeans, with buffet banquets on a long refectory table we had in the Mtwara Millennium Hotel. It was a very exciting time.

Dhow building harbour, Funguni, Zanzibar

Because no quantities are given in some of these recipes, and it is not possible to know exactly what the dominant flavours and the exact proportions of ingredients were in the past, I interpreted them according to my own taste. In all traditional countries where recipes are passed down by word of mouth or by watching and where no one uses weighing machines, precise recipes are rarely given and people are accustomed to trusting their taste and using their common sense. In my original roughly handwritten manuscript I included many of the recipes and I found years later that it had set a kind of fashion for Zanzibari banqueting, or Ramadhan *futari*, in certain academic circles. I was especially fascinated with the way my wife analysed and explained to me some of these recipes that existed more than seven hundred years ago. (Anyone who knows spices, taste, smell and the touch of dishes like biriani and pilau will have to agree with me that Zanzibar is a culinarily rich island).

I come from a famous Swahili and Islamist family. My uncle, Said Ilyas, was an intellectual, educated at Oxford University, who took care of me, after my mother died. I first started to be interested in preparing food at five years of age, and spent much of my free time running errands to small shops to buy different spices for my uncle's wife and my grandmother, who was in the kitchen fourteen hours a day.

I was born in 1949 of Comoran parents who migrated to Zanzibar. My father, a farmer, and my mother died when I was three years old. Thereafter my uncle, Mr Said Ilyas, took care of me. I left school at fourteen and worked for one year as a delivery boy and dish washer in a hotel called the Karthalla Hotel in the Comoroes, during which time I taught myself more about serving and cooking French dishes. At fifteen I asked my uncle to help me financially to leave Africa for Europe; but he refused, and I had to find my own way. In 1968 I left East Africa by cargo ship for Finland and worked as a galley boy. Now I really found myself dealing with cooking professionally, despite never having been to cookery school. At the same time I studied the Swedish language privately.

When the ship came to the Åland Islands in 1972 I disembarked and started studying Hotel and Restaurant Management full time. By the time tourism started to develop in the Åland Islands in the late 1970s I had finished my course as a chef. I felt isolated in the Åland Islands because I was the only African living in this tiny tourist paradise, but I stayed there anyway, despite the loneliness. I married and my first daughter, Fatma, was born in 1978; two more children were born later in Helsinki, and one in Dar es Salaam, where I was doing research into Swahili gastronomy. It was in 1988 that I started to become well known for my culinary articles in Finland, through *Helsingin Sanomat*, *Hufvudstadsbladet* and films on Finnish Television. I came at the subject from a sociological angle, because cookery was a subject that sociology had neglected.

Much of my work reflects my preoccupation with the African culinary world and its gastronomical and historical development. The history of cookery is to that extent a sideline. I was the source of countless written articles and contributions to Finnish newspapers and journals about African gastronomy. At the beginning of the 1990s, almost all big supermarkets in Helsinki had different products from Africa like coconut and octopus; alligator meat and ostrich fillet were served in the Hotel Intercontinental, Helsinki.

I studied more undiscovered culinary manuscripts. I became well known in the Finnish gastronomic community, and became more interested in African food history – a phenomenal esoteric store of knowledge which I much admired. But, back then, I had a great surprise. I loved Italian gastronomy and travelled to Rome and other big Italian cities to meet interesting chefs like Sabatini, Papa Giovanni, the son of Carbonara, and was invited to Rudolfo's restaurant as a guest of honour by his son on the occasion of his birthday.

I have been a linguist from the beginning, I loved English literature and I enjoyed writing. I possess dictionaries and grammars in about seven languages. My interest in linguistics, and especially the African languages, dates from my early teens. It was the richness of these languages, which I started studying on my own when I was fifteen, that drew me to this strange world in which I now live. I attended the Ålands Hotel and Restaurant Management College where I obtained my certificate as a chef, and the École de Ritz in Paris where I finished my gastronomy studies.

In 1998, under a programme sponsored by the Tanzanian Ministry of Education, I spent five years in Tanzania writing a Hotel and Restaurant Management syllabus for the whole country. I worked as consultant in Forodhani College, different private hotels in training, and became a good friend of the principal, Mrs Kibogoyo, who gave me more ideas about Swahili cuisine and how I could modernise it. This period was also an introduction to my New Swahili Cuisine and the beginning of my interest in the historical gastronomy of Zanzibar. During these years in Tanzania I visited Zambia, the Ivory Coast and Pemba, and since then I have travelled regularly in East Africa, also visiting Mombasa and Nairobi to discover their food.

I am particularly interested in the gastronomic aspect of the old recipes, and cook all the dishes to better understand them. I once prepared an East African gastronomy show in Paris, and many Japanese people were surprised when they tasted the different type of cuisine. I was later astonished to receive a call on 3 March 2005 from Shuji Shibata (Producer and Director for Nippon Television Network Corporation) of Sfinx Inc in Tokyo, inviting me to Tokyo to showcase my culinary arts at the Tokyo Broadcasting Corporation. The interesting thing was that I had only three days to prepare myself. But I did it. This extensive hands-on experience is one of the foundation stones of my great success as a food columnist and restaurant chef in Paris where, for many years, I reviewed everything from tiny Vietnamese noodle shops and barbecues run by Africans, to the grandest 'Jewish Cuisine' restaurants. To place dishes in their context and follow their development, I am not shy about using other intellectual disciplines – linguistics or political history (since many dishes have connections with royal courts) – as well as economic history in order to track something through recorded trade contacts.

I decided upon a change of environment after living and working for about thirty years in Europe, or let me put it this way, overseas. Therefore, I packed my bags, left Paris in April 1998, and went directly to Zanzibar.

During my first half year in Zanzibar, I really had a hard time, especially regarding the mentality of the society, to which I was not accustomed. I quarrelled with all the members of my family and I had to find my own way in the society to teach myself how to live with them.

In the second half year I did well and I became a jack-of-all-trades in my profession. I found life in Zanzibar could be busy, especially when I became my own boss.

Most of the recipes I have written down in this book are from the collections I had when I was living in Southern Tanzania – at Mtwara, where I spent more than half of my time writing. There, of course, I had the opportunity of learning by myself the way to live with the Swahili people.

Zanzibar and Pemba, islands with twelve hours of sun daily, possess a powerful allure, with their wide open spaces, in which the Zanzibaris carefully preserve their natural environment and ensure access to full-flavoured products from fishing, vegetables and animal breeding.

Zanzibari menus are simple and congenial. The dishes are often based on fish for everyday life and meat for special occasions. Dishes like *kuku wa kupaka* from the coast, and meat banana stew, are typical of a highly rich culinary culture, which deserves to be admired.

A big shark and fisherman

During my five-year stay in Zanzibar I have always enjoyed the lavish 'mama and sister' dishes at home. Nevertheless, what I enjoyed the most were the Ramadhan buffets which my wife and her mother cooked. Zanzibaris cuisine is not modern, but in the town and the popular *Forodhani*, near Beit El Ajaib, the dishes are lighter, spicier and more complex. A number of old chefs who once worked in the now defunct Zanzibar Hotel, Tembo Hotel, and Africa House, still cook, but they have never created any special dishes; they are still stuck with their traditional cookery, and adapt their raw products to the demands of an international cuisine.

Cooking and locally grown products are an integral part of the many festivities that take place in Zanzibar every year. At Ramadhan, the whole coast of East Africa fasts for the entire day and eats only in the evenings, at weddings, and at very special occasions, when their buffets are very delicious, served with *sambusa* and fish cutlets.

The subtle contrasts found in Zanzibari cooking invigorate both body and soul, which is why I am, and will always remain a great admirer of these tiny sun-blessed islands of Zanzibar and Pemba, and their culinary culture.

Some historians claim that Zanzibar got the name from *zenj*, a medieval Persian word for black people. Some of us do not agree with this claim. We believe that 'Zanzibar' originates in the word '*zingiber*', the ginger plant, which is plentiful in the islands and grows wild everywhere.

This herb, called *Zingiber officinale*, is native to south-eastern Asia, cultivated for its flavourful rhizome (underground stem or 'root'), which is used as a spice and as a medicine. Ginger root is used both fresh and in ground or powdered form, but the two forms are hardly substitutes for one another. Ginger was probably introduced to Africa via Eastern African connections to the Middle East and western Asia. Ginger is used as a spice all over Africa, and strong ginger drinks are especially popular in our Swahili culinary dishes. Some food experts see a connection between the words '*Zingiber*' and 'Zanzibar', as mentioned above.

The word '*Unguja*' – the Swahili name for Zanzibar – comes from *Ungo jaa*. The Arab settlers who visited the islands every now and then in their large dhows, using the monsoon winds, had the opportunity to fish going to and from the islands, and when they arrived at their destinations, they would announce, 'My *ungo* is full of fish' or '*Ungo wangu umejaa*.' The islands got their names from these culinary stories.

In this unknown heaven, when the wind blows in the right direction, the fragrance of spice is deliciously strong, and you know you are in Zanzibar. The Spice Islands of Zanzibar and Pemba, with their cloves and cinnamon, lychee nuts, cocoa beans, and coconuts, are tiny islands, part of Tanzania, the name deriving from a combination of the names of the two formerly separate states, Tanganyika and the Republic of Zanzibar.

The food market is in the middle of Zanzibar town, dividing the town into two parts. One is Ngambu and the other one is Stone Town, the older part. In the market, fruit and vegetables are abundant. Barefoot vendors in colourful balloon pants and skullcaps sit cross-legged on the ground before neat rows or piles of their products. Bananas and plantains, cassava, addoes (a potato-like vegetable), hot red peppers, and all kinds of green vegetables are in plentiful supply in their stalls.

Bags of coloured coconut, purple and pink, are found everywhere and are surprisingly delicious. Sticky sesame candy and hot baked sweet potatoes, toasted corn, and baked cassava are sold on the street. Boys with baskets made of palm leaves on their heads, carrying papayas, bananas and coconuts, are all around the market.

The rural culinary culture provided many interesting experiences. The delightful hospitality of the islanders is inexpressible. Gastronomy in an island like Pemba, for example, includes a silvery liquid shimmering with small round fish (somewhat like butterfish) in a luscious lemon-flavoured sauce. It is very appetising. The aroma of sweet potatoes baking on a three-stone hearth fills the air. The amazing coolness of the mud huts in the Pemba villages intrigues anyone who believes in an ecological lifestyle.

Breadfruit tree, Pemba Island

I owe Mama Kibogoyo and my wife, Ahyatt, a great and affection-ate debt for their advice, which inspired me in the early days of my research. But I did not have the opportunity to stay with Mama Kibogoyo long enough to complete this book before I had to leave East Africa.

Zanzibari food is now fashionable and popular in East Africa. Special ingredients and Zanzibari spices can be found in supermarkets. Zanzibari chefs have spread around the world now. Although the recipes in the book represent a kind of gastronomic archaeology, they are recipes you can cook from. Do try them, and use your own taste to interpret them. Knowing something about the ancient background of a dish adds to the pleasure of cooking and eating it, and is a thrilling way of understanding the world it comes from.

Contents

Fish and Seafood

Sweets and Desserts

Chutney

Starters

BANANA SALAD WITH BEETROOT AND POACHED EGG

Preparation time: 15 minutes

INGREDIENTS: SALAD

6 green hard bananas, blanched	*2 spring onions*
3 cooked beetroots	*50g green salad*
4 new potatoes	*2 tbs basil*
50g cooked mutton meat	*3 tbs peas, blanched*

INGREDIENTS: SAFFRON DRESSING

3 flowers dried Turkish saffron	*2 tbs white sugar*
2 egg yolks	*salt and pepper*
1 tbs red wine vinegar	*2dl corn oil[1]*

INGREDIENTS: POACHED EGGS

3 eggs	*1 tbs salt*
1l water	*2 tbs vinegar essence, spirit vinegar (12%)*

METHOD

Simmer the bananas, beetroots, new potatoes, and fresh peas in separate saucepans. Crisp-fry the pieces of meat.

Mix all the ingredients for the dressing except the oil. Add the oil a little at a time, while whisking to emulsify.

Bring the water to boil. Add the salt and vinegar essence. Break the eggs carefully into the water and simmer until they float to the surface. Lift out the eggs; chill them in ice water and drain on tissue paper.

Arrange the salad on the plate. Garnish with the beetroots. Spoon over the saffron dressing.

---

[1] For those who live in countries unfamiliar with the word decilitre (dl), it represents ten centilitres. So 2dl = 20 centilitres.

BANANA GRATIN

Preparation time: 15 minutes

INGREDIENTS: FRIED BANANAS

4 green bananas	*salt*
5 spoons cooking oil	*powdered Spanish red paprika*

INGREDIENTS: TOMATO CONCASSE

3 tomatoes	*2 leaves basil, chopped*
1 onion, chopped	*1dl olive oil*
2 cloves garlic, chopped	*3 big spoonsfuls emmental cheese,*
3 spoons concentrated tomato paste	*grated*
1dl white wine	

METHOD

After peeling the bananas, bisect them in the middle, spice them and crisp-fry until golden brown.

Sauté the onions, garlic, and crushed tomatoes. Mix the paste and the spices. Simmer the concasse and leave it until it is thick.

Arrange the bananas on the plate; pour the concasse on the bananas and the grated cheese on the top.

Bake it under the salamander or grill until golden brown cheese is formed. Garnish with a leaf of basil on the top.

STUFFED TOMATOES

Preparation time: 20 minutes

Serves 3–4

INGREDIENTS:

1 cup cooked coconut peas
large onion, chopped
1 tbs butter
salt
white pepper

6–8 stuffing tomatoes, tops removed
olive oil
2 tomatoes, peeled and chopped
HP sauce
¾ cup grated cheese

METHOD

Sauté onion in butter until cooked but not browned. Combine with cooked coconut peas.

Lightly rub outside of stuffing tomatoes with olive oil. Place in a baking pan in a single layer.

In each tomato put a thin layer of coconut peas. Cover with a layer of chopped tomatoes. Brush with HP sauce. Sprinkle cheese over tomato.

Repeat layers until all the tomatoes are filled.

Cover pan and bake at 350°C for 25 minutes. Remove cover and bake another 5 minutes.

Makonde Plateau Mushrooms

Preparation time: 15 minutes

Once I sat down at the beach side near the Millennium Village in Mtwara and I was approached by a gentleman. 'Benn, do you want some mushrooms?' I was shocked: mushrooms in Mtwara? I looked at the gentleman and replied, 'Yes, where are they?' He opened the basket he had: big white fresh lovely mushrooms. I just immediately thought if 'Le Nôtre' and Paul Bocuse knew that there are better mushrooms here than those of Paris, they would hang themselves.

The mushrooms come from down the mountains near Newala in Southern Mtwara about 40 km from Newala. The area is known as the Makonde Plateau. This is what I did to the mushrooms.

INGREDIENTS

500g Makonde mushrooms	*100–200 ml double heavy cream*
butter	*3 medium-sized cassavas*
salt and white pepper	*4 large red onions*

METHOD

The mushrooms – completely divided – are placed in a big frying pan to steam off the water. When the water is gone, once it has acted as a boiling or frying liquid, the mushrooms take up noticeably less room, and their taste becomes more concentrated. A few pats of butter and a little salt and white pepper draw out the delicious flavour of the mushrooms, and the cream gives them the right texture. I served these on slices of cassava. Peel the cassava; boil it in lightly salted water for 3 or 4 minutes.

These mushrooms may be cooked in sauce using butter, flour and a little cream. The Makonde mushrooms are almost too good to merit such brutal treatment. Moreover, if I add some soy sauce I hardly dare mention the fact.

GREEN PEA SOUP

Preparation time: 20 minutes

Kisutu market is one of the places I always visit when I am in Dar es Salaam. Here you can get fresh green peas all the year round. One day I went there on a Wednesday and it came to my mind that the next day would be Thursday, and I remembered the Finnish pea soup with pancakes that is eaten every Thursday in the army and in schools in Finland. I really missed that pea soup. But then, I couldn't prepare a pea soup like this in Finland! Anyway, I bought the fresh peas and went home. The following is what I prepared for a Dutch friend of mine who was director of the Veta Hotel in Dodoma, Mr Allard, who visited me that evening.

INGREDIENTS

1kg fresh green peas
1l mutton stock
5 tbs flour
1 red onion, chopped
150ml heavy cream

salt and white pepper
100ml Sandeman sherry
a few coriander leaves, chopped
broad-leafed parsley as garnish

METHOD

Boil the peas in the stock for about 10 minutes and blend the peas and stock in a food processor.

Shake the flour with a little bit of cold stock in a thickening bowl; add the chopped onions and the cream. Let the soup boil for at least 5 minutes to remove the taste of flour.

Season with salt, pepper, sherry and the freshly chopped coriander to give the soup a special character. Top off with sprig of parsley, for a fresh green contrast to the deeper, duller green of soup.

Serve the soup with *mikate ya kusukuma* (Swahili bread).

SHORBA BULGUR WHEAT SOUP

Preparation time: 35 minutes

Those who were living in Malindi in the 1950s and 60s before the revolution would be sure to hear the unmicrophoned muezzin of Alhabib Bajubeir five times a day calling people to go and pray in the Almasjid Jumma. I was one of the lucky kids who lived with his family in those years. This soup is a tribute to his late wife, Bi Masaad, who was in charge of preparing it in the month of Ramadhan. I was always near the casserole when it was prepared.

Now in my fifties and living in Finland, I cannot be without this soup in the month of Ramadhan. My dear friends, please try this recipe and you will enjoy your fasting!

INGREDIENTS

1kg beef bones with meat   *1½ level tsp salt*
2½ pints water   *½ cinnamon stick*
onion   *2 cardamom seeds*
2 cloves garlic   *3dl bulgur wheat or quick oats*
6 peppercorns   *juice of half a lemon*

METHOD

Put the bones, onions, garlic, peppercorns and salt in cold water. Bring to the boil.

Boil for half an hour, add the remaining spices and continue boiling for an hour.

Strain. Mix the bulgur wheat, or quick oats, and four tablespoons of stock and add the remaining stock.

Leave the porridge to cook well for about 10 to 20 minutes.

Simmer for about 10 minutes, add lemon juice and the meat with its bones. Serve it hot.

CHICKEN LIVER PÂTÉ SERVED WITH WARM PAPAYA SALSA

Preparation time: 15 minutes

INGREDIENTS: CHICKEN LIVER PÂTÉ

400g chicken liver	*1 clove of garlic, crushed*
salt and black pepper	*1dl sweet vermouth*
75g butter	

INGREDIENTS: PAPAYA SALSA

¼ of a pawpaw, chopped	*2 green limes, chopped*
1 bunch parsley, chopped	*honey*
2 hot chillies, chopped	*red vinegar*
3 fresh tomatoes, chopped	*olive oil*
1 fresh cucumber, chopped	

METHOD

Fry the chicken liver, but make sure it remains pink inside. Add salt, pepper and sweet vermouth. Blend the fried chicken liver with butter and chopped garlic in the food processor. Put the mixture in the bowl or terrine and leave it covered in the refrigerator for overnight if possible.

Mix all the ingredients together, then add the olive oil, vinegar, and honey. Warm the salsa when serving.

Opposite: Village hand crafts (women sewing baskets with dried coconut leaves) © Sultan Govani

Overleaf: Fishing dhows ready to start fishing trip © Sultan Govani

LOBSTER CREAM WITH FRESH PAPAYA

Preparation time: 30 minutes

Many times I've sat down and thought about this fruit, the pawpaw, and tried to find it a special place of its own with seafood. At last when I was in Mtwara in 2000 just near the beach I was approached by a young boy of ten years old, and he had both products: fresh lobster and very lovely ripe pawpaw. I bought the lobster and he offered me the pawpaw free of charge. The following recipe was the result.

INGREDIENTS

2½ cups cooked lobster meat, chopped
¼ cup mayonnaise
1 tbs fresh chillies, minced
1 tbs fresh parsley, minced
1 tsp fresh lime juice
⅛ tsp salt

⅛ tsp freshly ground green pepper granules
½ cup heavy cream, whipped
1 ripe papaya, peeled, seeded and thinly sliced
fresh mint sprigs (garnish).

METHOD

Combine mayonnaise, chillies, lime juice, parsley, salt, and pepper in a small bowl.

Fold in whipped cream. Add lobster and papaya. Mix gently.

Garnish with fresh mint. Serve immediately.

My Lover's Lobster

Preparation time: 20 minutes

This lobster I did for my wife on her birthday, and it was such a big success, I could not believe it myself. It happened that I was just joking with her. Instead of going to a restaurant I told her I would do the special meal myself.

INGREDIENTS

1½ cups heavy cream
3 each egg yolks, well beaten
½ tsp salt
¼ tsp Zanzibar green pepper granules

⅛ tsp local Zanzibar hot cayenne pepper
3 cups cooked lobster meat, finely diced
1 tbs butter
2 tbs sherry (optional)

METHOD

Over hot water, heat cream. Stir in egg yolks and seasonings. Stir until mixture starts to thicken.

Add lobster, butter and sherry. Cook one minute longer over hot water.

Serve on toast corners or in puff pastry shells. It may be served hot or cold.

CHILLED LOBSTER AND MUSSEL COCKTAIL WITH CURRY DRESSING

Preparation time: 15 minutes

INGREDIENTS

12 champagne glasses
1 head romaine salad, julienne strips
1½kg lobster, cooked, diced

1½kg mussels, poached (court bouillon)
mint sprigs (garnish)

SAUCE

1 cup mayonnaise
*2 cups sour cream (*mtindi *or* Russian *smetana)*
1½ tbs Zanzibar curry powder

2–3 tbs English mango chutney
1 tbs horseradish (optional)
½ tsp fresh lime or lime zest

METHOD

Lay the salad in champagne glasses. Distribute the seafood over greens. Sauce fish at service and garnish with mint sprigs. Serve it cold.

Green Mix with Indian Ocean Sea Fruits

Preparation time: 15 minutes

Every morning in Mtwara I would sit nearby the seaside. The Millennium Village was built in such a way that I could watch the early morning sunrise and the evening sunset. At both times the fishermen passed close by the hotel when sailing to their destination. That meant I was always the first to buy the catch of the day. It happened that one day I got a surprise. I bought a lot of seafood in the morning just in case, but the surprise I got was at noon when I saw a delegation from the Japanese Embassy at Dar es Salaam who had come to Mtwara. They insisted on a quick lunch for thirteen people. I did not have any salad or bread, but I had coastal Swahili doughnuts prepared with coconut cream, which are known as *maandazi*, and so I was in a panic. I love exotic food and I like experimenting. I always see that my experiment is audacious.

Here is what they had for a starter at lunchtime.

SALAD

1kg cooked spinach	4kg various cooked seafood, including:
1 pce lettuce	• prawns
2 bottles capers	• octopus
3dl mayonnaise	• blackfish
3 bunches fresh dill	• abalones
	• kingfish
	• mussels

MAYONNAISE

5 egg yolks	salt and white pepper
1 tsp mustard	1l neutral oil
2 tsp vinegar	

Maandazi (Swahili Doughnuts)

Preparation time: 45 minutes

INGREDIENTS

1l heavy coconut cream	*4 tbs sugar*
2dl heavy fresh cream or fresh milk	*700g Bakharesa white flour*
3 tbs ghee	*2 tbs dry granule yeast or*
1 tsp cardamom	*50g fresh yeast*
a pinch of cinnamon, a pinch of salt	

METHOD

Mix the cream and coconut cream together. Warm the mixture to the temperature of about 60°C; stir the yeast into the mixture. Mix the ghee, sugar, a pinch of salt, cardamom, cinnamon and finally the flour. Knead together and leave to rise for 30 minutes. Prepare your balls of doughnuts and leave them to rise for 30 minutes again before you deep-fry them to golden brown.

Mix all the green vegetables and seafood together.

All the ingredients should be at room temperature. Blend the egg yolk, mustard, vinegar and seasoning. Add the oil with care, drop by drop to start with and then a bit faster, so the mayonnaise does not curdle.

Arrange your plate. Put the half doughnut on the plate and the green mix on it, place the half doughnut on the top, and serve it with cold South African white wine.

SAFFRON SPICED MUSSEL SOUP

Preparation time: 15 minutes

INGREDIENTS

2 tbs margarine	*1dl heavy coconut cream*
2 chopped red onions	*1 pkt Turkish saffron*
24 cleaned fresh Zanzibar	*juice of half a lemon*
mussels with shells	*salt and fresh grounded black pepper*
1dl red wine vinegar	*fresh green coriander, chopped*
2 yellowish egg yolks	*½ litre fish stock*

METHOD

Fry the onions in margarine for a couple of minutes.

Add the red wine and lemon juice.

Add the mussels to cook under lock for 5 minutes until the mussels open.

Shake the casserole well and often.

Take out the mussels and keep them warm. Strain the liquid and put it back in the casserole.

Whip in the egg yolks, coconut cream and Turkish saffron. Let it cook a bit while mixing well until the soup is a little thick. Spice it with salt and black pepper.

Put the warm mussels on the soup plate to serve and add the soup over. Garnish with chopped fresh coriander.

Serve the soup with *mikate ya kusukuma*.

Opposite: Village bachelor cottages © Sultan Govani
Overleaf: Local dhow repair yard © Sultan Govani

Morning Octopus Soup

Preparation time: 20 minutes

I received many dignitaries in Mtwara, but this day when I prepared this soup I thought people would laugh at me. I must say that my stay in the Åland Islands at Mariehamn in Finland gave me a lot of experience in preparing seafood. Here on the Tanzanian coast, people do not have the same culinary culture as in Mariehamn, but the morning smell is the same. However, in the Baltic, the fish are not the same as in the Indian Ocean.

One morning I received the Finnish Ambassador from Dar es Salaam, who had not had breakfast. Although Mtwara is a big town, not everything is available; we had to depend on everyday local products rather than international products. This day I had another problem: I had to prepare breakfast for the Ambassador.

In short, in Baltic countries, people have soup during the day, like pea soup on Thursday, or in the evening as a starter, but here in the Swahili diet culture and special culinary philosophy, people have soup for breakfast, and so I invited the Ambassador to a Swahili breakfast with Octopus Soup as a starter.

INGREDIENTS: SOUP

1kg cooked octopus   *salt, pepper, chillies*
2 red onions, chopped   *1dl white wine*
1 clove of garlic, chopped *1 clove and a pinch of cinnamon*
2 fresh tomatoes, chopped   *1l fish stock*
1 bunch spinach, chopped

METHOD

Cut the octopus into small pieces and shallow-fry them in butter, pour on the fish stock and season to taste. Add the finely chopped ingredients and simmer the soup for about 10 minutes before serving. Garnish the soup with chopped dill.

Serve the soup with Swahili chapatis, pawpaw and Zanzibar masala tea.

Of course, in cold countries you can serve this soup as a starter according to local culinary conventions.

COASTAL PRAWN SOUP WITH COCONUT CREAM

Preparation time: 15 minutes

I prepared this soup in 1989 in Helsinki. There was a programme called *Good Morning Finland* on the TV and the producer wanted an exotic recipe for that morning. Anyway, she approached the right person. Of course, I knew that most Finns did not know what a coconut was in those days; despite that, you could find them in Stockman, the most exclusive supermarket in Helsinki at that time. They asked me to choose where I wanted to do the programme. I phoned a girlfriend of mine who was working as a restaurant manager in the Tiger Restaurant near Esplanade Street, and she agreed, of course. I told her to order the following ingredients:

400g cooked prawns	*2 crushed garlic cloves*
2 coconuts	*chilli powder*
1 red onion	*curry powder*
cinnamon powder	*salt, pepper*

METHOD

Peel the prawns, cut them into pieces and let them boil until soft in the cream of coconut. Blend in the food processor along with a little bit of fish stock. The more prawns you use the thicker soup will be. Season the soup and add the rest of ingredients. Leave the soup to simmer for about 5 minutes.

Garnish the soup with completely peeled prawn and a petal of dill.

This soup became very popular among the local people in Mtwara. When one of my friends, Mr Msuya, came to visit me he always wanted this soup, and wanted only me to prepare it. If somebody else prepared this soup he'd get the feeling that the taste was not the same. In addition, of course, he would come to ask in the kitchen, 'Who prepared the soup?' and shout, 'Where is Benn?'

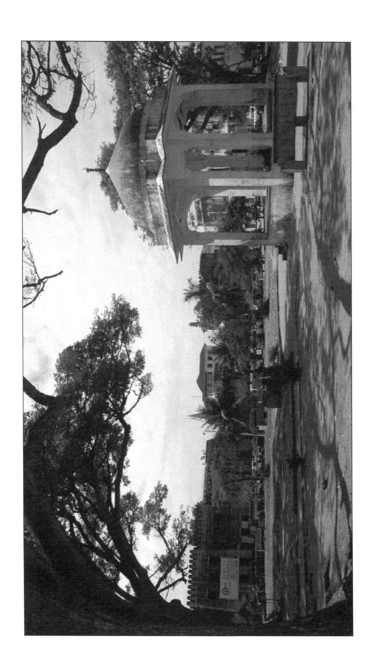

CUCUMBER RING

Preparation time: 15 minutes

INGREDIENTS

4 leaves of gelatine or 1 spoon of   *white pepper*
gelatine powder   *fresh basil, chopped*
1 pce cucumber (about 400g)   *home-made yoghurt (*mtindi)
juice of lime
salt

METHOD

Put the gelatine leaves in cold water.

Peel the cucumber and take out the seeds by using a spoon. Grate it and season the grated cucumber with lime juice, salt and pepper.

Melt the gelatine in a saucepan with very little water on a low heat. Mix the lukewarm liquid well with grated cucumber. Pour into a ring-shaped tin that has been rinsed with cold water. Put into the refrigerator for a few hours or overnight.

Turn out onto a plate. Fill the hole in the ring with fresh yoghurt spiced with fresh shredded basil, salt, pepper and lime juice.

Serve it very cold with Swahili roast beef.

Sweet Potato Soup

Preparation time: 20 minutes

INGREDIENTS

*1kg red, light red or rose sweet
potato
1l chicken stock
3 tbs concentrated tomato purée*

*salt
white pepper
a little bit of sugar*

METHOD

Peel the sweet potatoes, cut them into pieces and let them boil until soft in the chicken stock.

Blend them in the food processor along with little stock, and mix the purée into the rest of the stock. The more sweet potatoes you use, the thicker the soup will be.

Beat in the tomato purée, season with a pinch of salt, pepper and sugar for taste.

Add cream to taste. Simmer the soup and serve it hot.

SAMBUSA

Preparation time: 1½ hours

Perhaps this is the best-known starter in the world. It is not only known in Asia but also in small states like Azerbaijan, Kazakhstan, etc.

Zanzibar *Sambusas* are very simple to prepare and those who are professional in preparing have trained many years.

INGREDIENTS: PASTRY

2 cups wholewheat flour   *a pinch of salt*

METHOD

Sieve the flour and salt together. Knead into a soft dough using water. Divide the dough into eight equal portions. Roll out each round into 150 mm (6") diameter chapatis. Cook on a frying pan for few seconds on both sides and set aside.

INGREDIENTS: FILLING

1 onion, very finely chopped   *2 tbs chopped coriander*
a pinch of cardamom   *juice of half a lemon*
a pinch of salt   *1 tbs oil*
1 cup fried minced meat   *oil for deep frying*
1 tsp green chilli-ginger paste

FILLING METHOD

Heat the oil in a pan, add the onion and sauté till golden in colour.

Add the minced meat, green chilli-ginger paste, sugar, lemon juice and salt and mix well. Cover and cook for 5 minutes on a slow flame.

Remove from the heat, add the coriander and mix well.

Cool and keep aside.

Divide each pastry sheet into two halves. Make a cone from each part and stuff with the filling. Seal the edges carefully using a little water. Repeat with the remaining pastry sheets and filling.

Deep-fry in hot oil of 60°C, but keep heating the oil to 100°C till golden brown in colour.

Serve the *sambusa* cold or hot.

KACHORI (WITH POTATOES)

Preparation time: 1 hour

Makes 12 kachoris

DOUGH

2 cups cooked mashed potatoes
½ tsp salt
1 tsp cumin seeds
1 tsp green chilli-ginger paste
1 tsp chilli powder

1 tsp garam masala
2 tbs flour
3 cups oil
salt to taste

OTHER INGREDIENTS

oil for deep frying

METHOD

Combine all the ingredients and knead into a firm dough. Knead very well for 5 to 7 minutes.

Add the green chilli-ginger paste, chilli powder, garam masala, and salt, and mix well.

Divide the dough into 12 equal parts and keep covered under a wet muslin cloth.

Heat the oil in a pan and add the cumin seeds and asafoetida.

Cool and divide into 12 equal portions. Shape each portion into a ball and keep aside.

Roll out each portion of the dough into a ball of 50 mm (2") diameter. Roll each in the flour and then the beaten eggs.

Heat the oil in a pan and add the cumin seeds. Deep-fry in the low heat until golden brown colour.

Cool and keep aside.

Serve hot or cold.

CRÊPES

METHOD

Mix in the water, flour, egg...
the ingredients together t...
very thick, add a little ...
Strain the mixt...
Warm up y...
When the pa...
cover the...
difficu...

i) Crêpes (*Mikate ya Maji*)

Preparation time: 15 minutes

This name 'crêpes' is French, as in crêpes Suzette, but I think I will put the name into English: Crêpes *Zenj* (meaning *mikate ya maji*, or water bread). Although Zanzibar does not have much of a baking culture, the island's gastronomy is very much coloured by different cultures, from Portuguese to Iranian. When I was in Lisbon in April 1974, I happened to eat these crêpes made with water and onions, just as we prepare in Zanzibar, and was surprised; but then I came to know that the chef who prepared the crêpes was from the town of Porto, where they prepare crêpes using water instead of milk.

INGREDIENTS

250g flour	*a pinch of salt*
4 eggs	*50g margarine or ghee or oil.*
½ l water	

..., salt and melted margarine. Whisk
... thoroughly. If you feel that the mixture is
... bit of water.
...re.
...ur pan and drop a small amount of margarine.
... is very hot, fry your first crêpe. The mixture should
... whole pan. Normally the first crêpe always has a few
...ties, but then the second and the rest become normal.
...The first crêpe will show you whether you have too much
water or your mixture is too thick. This always depends on what
kind of flour you have used.

Fry your crêpes both sides until golden brown.

Do not use any oil or margarine in the process of frying the
crêpes because you have already mixed the margarine into the
mixture.

TIPS FOR KEEPING YOUR FRYING PAN CLEAN.

- Never clean your crêpe frying pan with soap, or your
  crêpes will stick when frying.

- Always clean your frying pan using only water and a brush;
  or

- Use coconut fibres (*makumbi*) to rub the pan after frying
  your crêpes; or

- Use kitchen paper roll to clean your frying pan.

ii) Onion Crêpes (*Mikate ya Maji na Vitunguu*)

Preparation time: 15 minutes

INGREDIENTS

2 red onions	*sugar*
a pinch of salt	*1 spoon oil or margarine*

METHOD

Chop your onions finely, and sauté. Add salt and a pinch of sugar
while frying the onions, so that they have a golden colour. Mix
the onions with your crêpe mixture and fry the crêpes.

iii) Minced Meat Crêpes (*Mikate ya Maji na Nyama ya Kusaga*)

INGREDIENTS

250g minced meat   *1 spoon oil*
salt, pepper

METHOD

Fry your minced meat until golden brown, salt and pepper it, and spice with a pinch of freshly chopped garlic. Mixed it with the crêpe mixture and fry your crêpes.

MBAAZI ZA NAZI (PEAS IN COCONUT MILK)

Mbaazi za Nazi is the traditional Swahili way to prepare this popular tropical pulse. The best chef I saw in my life preparing this dish is Bi Khadija wa Sheikh (Mwenye Enzi Mungu Amrehemu). She was living at Vikokotoni near the mosque called Msikiti Nambari. I remember very well, I was coming almost every morning to buy mandaazi (Swahili doughnuts) and peas with coconut. In the 1950s and 60s this dish was sold early in the morning in different houses by different ladies in Zanzibar. It was a dish eaten with bread or doughnuts as breakfast.

INGREDIENTS

1kg pigeon peas (dried); or substitute black-eyed peas, yellow-eyed peas or cowpeas, cleaned, soaked, and rinsed
1/2 cups each of 'thick' and 'thin' coconut milk.

oil or margarine or ghee
1/2 onions, chopped
1 hot green chilli pepper, cleaned and chopped
1 tsp curry powder or turmeric
salt, to taste

METHOD

In a large pot, combine pigeon peas and just enough water to cover. Bring to the boil, reduce heat, cover, and simmer until the peas begin to become tender and most of the water is absorbed. There are so many ways of cooking peas. In the traditional way, Bi Khadija would use a branch of banana to boil the peas with. The branch of banana consists of liquid which acts like bicarbonate, quickening the cooking process of the peas, and also it adds a special taste.

Stir in the thin coconut milk. Continue to simmer over a low heat. Add more water as necessary to prevent the peas from becoming dry.

While peas are simmering, heat a few tablespoons of oil or ghee. Add the curry powder and a little bit of turmeric and stir for a minute.

Fry the onion and chilli pepper until they are tender.

Combine the peas and onion–chilli mixture (add either one to the other). Continue to simmer until the peas are tender enough to eat.

Add the thick coconut milk and simmer on the lowest possible heat for 5 to 10 minutes, stirring occasionally.

Serve the peas with doughnuts.

LOBSTER COCKTAIL WITH FRESH ORANGE SALSA

Preparation time: 45 minutes

INGREDIENTS

2 tbs yellow peppers, diced small
1 tbs green peppers
2 tbs onion finely chopped
$^1/_2+$ of a jalapeño pepper, seeded and finely minced (depending on amount of heat)
1 medium tomato, seeded, drained and diced
$^1/_4$ cucumber, diced small
$1^1/_2$ tbs finely minced mint
3 tbs of finely minced cilantro

1 tbs of extra virgin olive oil
2 key limes, juice only
3 tbs of fresh orange juice, about $^1/_2$ small orange
salt and pepper
1 Maine lobster (approx 1.3 pounds), cooked rare, coarsely chopped
1 medium Zanzibar avocado, diced into cubes

METHOD

Make a salsa by combining yellow and green peppers, onion, jalapeño, tomato, cucumber, mint, cilantro, olive oil, juice of 1 lime, and a half of the orange juice with a pinch of salt and pepper to taste.

Marinate the lobster meat in the remaining lime juice and orange juice for 5 minutes, check seasonings.

Take a chilled Martini glass, put a small amount of salsa in the bottom of the glass. Arrange a layer of lobster meat on top, and add a layer of the diced avocado. Repeat the process until the glass is almost full. End with a layer of lobster on top, and top it with a small teaspoon of salsa and avocado. You now have a refreshingly light appetiser full of tropical flavours.

Opposite: Stone Town streets © Sultan Govani
Overleaf: Sunset in Zanzibar town © Sultan Govani

LOBSTER SAMOSAS SERVED WITH TAMARIND SAUCE

Preparation time: 1½ hour

INGREDIENTS

2 cups lobster meat, chopped
2 tbs shallots, finely chopped
3 tbs marinated sun-dried
tomatoes, finely chopped
¾ cup firm ripe avocado, diced

2 tsp fresh lemon juice
8 pastry roll wrappers
1 each egg, beaten
2 cups coconut oil for frying

METHOD

Mix lobster, shallots, tomatoes, avocado and lemon juice, tossing gently to combine. Divide mixture into eight portions. With one wrapper corner pointing toward you, brush edges with egg and place filling about 1" from bottom corner and 1" from each side. Fold up triangle-style, sealing filling firmly. Refrigerate for 30 minutes.

Heat oil in a deep pan or wok over a medium–high heat. When the oil is hot, fry two rolls at a time for about 3 to 4 minutes or until golden. Drain on paper towels. To serve, cut each roll in half on the diagonal. Place on individual lettuce-lined plates and serve with dipping sauce. Garnish with cilantro.

INGREDIENTS: TAMARIND SAUCE:

¼ cup light seasoned balsamic vinegar
1 tbs fresh ginger, grated
1 clove fresh garlic, chopped
½ tsp salt

3 tbs limeade concentrate, thawed
½ tsp fresh Zanzibar tamarind concentrate or pulp
½ cup fresh cilantro, firmly packed
¼ cup roasted Mtwara cashew nuts
½ cup plus 2 tsp light olive oil.

METHOD

Combine all ingredients except the oil in a food processor or blender until chopped. With the motor running, add the oil and process until blended. Refrigerate for at least four hours or overnight for best flavour.

Main Dishes

Mutton Casserole with Tropical Fruits

A warm casserole with tropical fruits is very well suited to a hot tropical country like Tanzania. In this version, brisket, shoulder or chops are all good for casserole. The bones heighten the taste and give a good consistency.

Everybody eats 'mutton' (goat meat) in Tanzania. They have strict rules for eating it. The paradox is that what the gourmet considers genuine mutton is actually the result of a food fiddle going back to our grandfathers. In those days, mutton was a delicacy for the rich and only used for ceremonies. Slaughtering goat at any time you wanted was considered uneconomical and not traditional.

Make more than you will be eating at one sitting. It tastes even better when it has been allowed to stand. And you'll have the pleasure of using the biggest iron pot.

With the right guests, you can ring any number of changes on mutton casserole: with vegetables or without vegetables, strongly spiced or just with onions and garlic… you will always make a delicious and attractive meal with mutton. It is a way of travelling, bringing back memories and taking others with you to distant places. Of course, my aim is to keep to the taste as a show of loyalty to Tanzania, but what would Tanzanian cuisine be without inspiration from abroad? Tanzanians are the only people today who have discovered the delights of foreign flavours.

Mutton Casserole

Preparation time: 1 hour

INGREDIENTS

1½kg mutton on the bone
olive oil
500g onions
2dl lime juice
3 chopped cloves of garlic or more
3 sticks of cinnamon

4 hot chillies
5 bay leaves
1 bunch mint
½l mutton stock
salt, black pepper and fresh ginger
½ pawpaw and 500g jackfruit

METHOD

Cut the meat into suitable portions and marinate the pieces in olive oil, lime juice and all the herbs and spices, for about four hours, or overnight.

Put all this together in an iron pot, and fill up with stock so that it covers the ingredients. Boil gently for about an hour.

Add the fruit to the pot and leave it to simmer for about 10 minutes. Serve the dish with coconut rice and very cold rosé wine.

Summer Fillet Steak

Preparation time: 15 minutes

This dish I prepared in a hotel outside Dar es Salaam called Beachcomber. It is a very small lovely hotel; I liked its position and the way it was built. Because it was artistic I decided to create an artistic menu to match it. This was one of the main courses I produced.

INGREDIENTS: BOILED FILLET OF BEEF IN RED WINE

300g fillet of beef
1 big onion spiked with Zanzibar
dried cloves
3 stock cubes

4 bay leaves
5 allspice and white peppercorns
6dl red wine
coriander stock

METHOD

Pour the wine and a little water into the saucepan, add the fillet of beef and boil for 10 minutes with the lid on. The stock should not cover the fillet. The total cooking time is only 12 minutes. It has to be juicy and show a nice pink colour inside. Serve the fillet with coriander stock.

Pour the stock from the fillet of beef in a saucepan, add chopped fresh green coriander leaves, stir it and serve.

BENN'S HONEY CHICKEN

INGREDIENTS: CHICKEN

1 chicken   *salt and black pepper*
olive oil

INGREDIENTS: SWEET POTATOES

500g sweet potatoes   *6 sliced cloves of garlic*
2 tbs olive oil for frying   *salt*
lime juice
INGREDIENTS: CARDAMOM YOGHURT

300 ml fresh yoghurt   *salt and black pepper*
1 tsp cardamom grounded seeds
INGREDIENTS: LIME HONEY

Peel and juice of three limes   *7 tbs honey*

METHOD

Set the oven at 225 °centigrade. Peel the sweet potatoes and cut them in halves lengthways or sliced. Turn them in olive oil, salt, sugar, garlic and lime juice in an ovenproof dish.

Salt and pepper the whole chicken. Sauté in olive oil to give it the colour. Transfer the chicken to an ovenproof dish with the sweet potatoes and roast until the juices run clear and the sweet potatoes are soft but slightly al dente with an attractive colour.

Mix the yoghurt with the cardamom, salt, and pepper to taste. Pour the mixture on the chicken; leave the chicken in the oven for 10 minutes more.

Carefully cut away all the white from the lime peel. Shred the peel finely and blanch in boiling water for a half minute. Simmer the juice and the peel in a saucepan for a minute. Stir in the honey and simmer for about a minute until it thickens.

Pour the lime honey over the chicken and serve.

Opposite: Historical slave chambers © Sultan Govani
Overleaf: Outside local Domino Café at Malindi © Sultan Govani

Chicken-Comber

Preparation time: 15 minutes

INGREDIENTS

2 skinless chicken breasts	*3 tomatoes, chopped*
3 tbs olive oil	*1 tbs fresh ginger, crushed*
2 tbs lime juice	*1 tbs fresh garlic, crushed*
1 tsp fresh cilantro leaves, chopped	*3 fresh ripe mangoes, chopped*
	1 chilli
1 fresh green chilli, finely chopped	*salt*
2 tbs sunflower oil	*1 dl fresh cream*
7 curry leaves or madras curry powder	*1 dl chicken stock*
	2 chopped red onions

METHOD

Rinse the chicken breasts and pat them dry. Remove the fillets and flatten the breasts. Using a sharp knife, make two diagonal slits on each breast to allow the flavours and heat to penetrate the flesh more easily.

In a small bowl, mix the olive oil, lemon juice and a little salt. Using a pastry brush, brush the mixture all over the breasts and chill.

Heat the sunflower oil in a saucepan over a moderate heat, fry the chopped onions and curry leaves for about 30 seconds. Then add the tomatoes and mangoes and fry for about 2 minutes. Finally, add the fresh cream and remove from the heat to keep warm.

Preheat the frying pan and fry the chicken breasts for 3 to 4 minutes on either side, until light golden, basting occasionally.

Serve the chicken on a warm plate, with sauce poured all around it, and garnished with the cilantro and green chillies. If you like, you can cut the breasts across at an angle into slices, then fan the slices out.

SUNNY MUTTON LEG

Preparation time: 1½ hours

I prepared this dish on my third weekend in Tanzania. I was in Zanzibar, at a small beach village called Chwaka. In this village there was a sweet little hotel called the Chwaka Beach Hotel. They had a lovely kitchen but no cook. I was there as a guest, and I had a beautiful friend with me to spend the weekend together. We were hungry, of course, and so we went to prepare some food for ourselves. It was lucky that we were permitted to use the kitchen. Moreover, we also got some meat, but there was nothing else except pineapple and green bananas. The following is what I prepared on that sunny weekend.

INGREDIENTS

1 boneless mutton leg	2 tbs soy sauce
3 sunflower oil	1 pce pineapple
4 pce fresh ginger root, grated	2dl pineapple juice
1 red chilli, seeded and finely	3dl mutton stock
chopped	4 pce raw corn
2 tsp allspice powder (in	salt and pepper, small-grained and
Swahili, pilau spices)	chopped
1 tbs sherry vinegar	

METHOD

Preheat the oven to 325°C.

Trim away any visible fat from the mutton leg.

Brush the sunflower oil over the base of a frying pan. Heat over a medium flame, and then fry the leg for about 2 minutes, until lightly browned.

Blend together the ginger, chilli, and allspice powder, vinegar and soy sauce.

Cut the pineapples into square chunks, reserving the juice. Prepare the stock with the juice, mix together with the spices and pour over the mutton leg.

Put the mutton leg in the oven tray, together with maize corn and roast for about one hour.

Take out the stock and strain in saucepan. Blend the corn starch with one tablespoon of cold water and gradually stir. Add to the mutton leg and the maize corn.

Serve it as it is with the maize corn.

MUTTON PILAU

Preparation time: 2 hours

Any tourist who arrives in Zanzibar should taste this dish. Many people think that the pilau dish in Zanzibar comes from India, but pilau, sometimes called pilaf rice, is in fact originally from Iran. It was probably brought to the island by the first Persian settlers on Zanzibar – like the Shiraz family, Mr Hassan bin Ali and his six sons who came to Tanzania in AD 950.

Groups of these settlers lived in Zanzibar, the Comoro Islands, Mombasa and in Bagamoyo, where the ruins are still there and can be seen.

INGREDIENTS: PILAU

1kg basmati rice
½kg mutton meat
3 pce Maggi cube
1kg red onions, sliced
4 pce potatoes
5 pce cooked eggs
200g almonds
200g raisins

2 tbs pilau masala powder or allspice
salt, pepper, cloves, crushed ginger,
completely cinnamon, cardamom
granules, crushed garlic
6 tbs ghee
7 tbs flour
8dl water

INGREDIENTS: TOMATO SALSA (*KACHUMBAR*)

9 fresh red tomatoes
10 red onions, sliced
1 bunch coriander, chopped
1 green salad or figili *(white radish salad), chopped*

1 dl lime juice
2 pce hot chillies
1dl red vinegar
1dl honey
2 cloves garlic, chopped

METHOD

Put the meat in cold water. Let it come to the boil for a few minutes. Put the seasonings into a little muslin bag. The mutton meat needs to be boiled well for 1½ hours or more.

Heat the casserole with ghee inside and start frying the potatoes until they are golden in colour. Add your onions, and sauté them nicely while mixing the rest of the spices. Mix the basmati rice with the meat and add the stock. Simmer the pilau very slowly with the lid on, while checking every now and then that it is not burnt.

Finish the dish by adding the almonds, raisins and cooked eggs.

Mix the flour with water, put it on the lid, and stick the lid on the casserole. Finish the cooking in the oven.

Wash the sliced red onions in warm water and mix them with the chopped tomatoes, salad, chillies, honey and vinegar. Add the lime juice and season the salsa.

Serve the pilau in a clay pot and garnish with raisins and almonds. Do not forget the salsa.

BIRIANI

Preparation time: 2 hours

Various biriani rice dishes are common in the cuisine of India and neighbouring countries. Swahili cuisine has biriani showing influences from both Arabia and India. The original Zanzibar biriani is much more Iranian in taste rather than Asian. As with pilau rice, it was probably Shirazi settlers who introduced biriani to Zanzibar around AD 950.

The origin of biriani is not very clear, but it is believed that, the first people to cook biriani were gypsies from Spain, who got the idea from the Moors. The Moors from Turkey and Iran, and Muslims from North Africa, invaded the Iberian peninsula early in the eighth century and drove deep into France but were turned back by Charles Martel at the Battle of Tours in 732. The Muslims retreated across the Pyrenees, firmly entrenching themselves for several hundred years in what is now Spain.

The Moors introduced rice into Islamic Spain, which was among the most civilised places on the planet, renowned for its scientists, philosophers, artists, architects, poets, musicians, herbalists and culinary experts.

There are still monuments to this civilisation in Alhambra, Almeria and Andalusia. The gypsies, some of whom married Muslims and became Muslims, cooked their dishes with rice using dried saffron flowers. In Valencia, when it was populated with gypsies, the dish was named 'Paella Valencia'.

The method of cooking paella is just like that used for biriani, but instead of using a dish they use a pan which is called a paella. The dish is popular from the Alhambra up to the French beach resort of Nice.

INGREDIENTS

10ms dried Turkish saffron flowers	*1kg potatoes cut in big cubes*
4 cloves garlic (minced)	*½ tsp cardamom grains*
1 tsp minced fresh ginger	*6 whole cloves*
1½kg meat (mutton, beef, goat, or	*5 pce cinnamon sticks*
chicken) cut into serving sized pieces	*1 tsp cumin seeds*
2 cups sour milk or plain yoghurt	*1 tsp coriander seeds*
2dl fresh lime juice	*½ tsp whole black peppercorns*
3dl red vinegar	*salt*
50g peeled almonds	*3 spoons pilau masala mix*
4 hard boiled eggs	*4 ripe peeled tomatoes, chopped*
5–4 spoons ghee	*1 small can tomato paste*
1kg red onions, finely sliced	*5 cups of rice*

METHOD

Heat oil in a large skillet. Deep-fry the onions in hot oil until they are golden brown. Remove from the skillet and set aside. Deep-fry the potatoes in the same oil until golden brown. Remove the potatoes and set them aside. Do not throw away the oil from the skillet; you will need it.

Boil the meat apart. Strain and keep aside.

Sauté all the spices using the oil from the skillet. Place the mixture in a large pot, add yoghurt or buttermilk and lime juice, cover and let it cook over low heat, stirring regularly. Add chopped tomatoes, tomato paste and few spoonfuls of oil from the skillet. Stir and continue to cook over low heat. Add bouillon from the cooked meat if the sauce becomes too thick. Season to taste with salt; add meat, potatoes and red vinegar. Simmer the dish until the potatoes and the meat are cooked. Finish the sauce by adding the dried saffron flowers.

Cook rice in the usual way (one part rice to two parts water) with a little bit of oil from the skillet. The meat should be done by the time the rice is cooked. Pre-heat oven to medium heat.

Cover the biriani sauce with the cooked rice. Mix 1dl cold water with the remaining dried saffron, and pour it on the rice. Put some dried raisins, peeled almonds and cooked eggs in the biriani. Cover it and bake it a little bit in the oven for about 20 minutes before you serve it.

Serve your biriani hot with traditional Zanzibar *kachumbar*.

MCHUZI WA KIMA (MINCED MEAT STEW)

Preparation time: 35 minutes

Perhaps the name of this stew is a little bit extraordinary. I sometimes wonder why it is called this, but I haven't got an answer yet. What makes the name extraordinary is that *kima* means 'monkey'. But this is one of my favourite dishes in the Ramdhan buffet.

INGREDIENTS

4 tbs ghee	*salt and pepper*
2 small red onions, finely chopped	*pinch of nutmeg, cloves and ginger*
5 potatoes finely chopped in cubes	*3 cloves chopped garlic*
1 bay leaf	*1 tsp lime juice*
¾kg ground beef	*1 tsp red vinegar*
1 tin tomato purée	*a pinch of cinnamon and*
½ cup beef stock	*cardamom*
½ tsp curry powder	

METHOD

In a large pot melt the butter and gently sauté the chopped onions, potatoes, and bay leaf for 8 to 10 minutes. Add ground beef, increase the heat slightly and cook until golden brown.

Taste for salt before seasoning. Add nutmeg tomato purée and half the stock or Maggi cube (with a cup of water) and simmer over a low heat, covered for 1½ hours.

Stir from time to time and add the remaining stock while adding the remainder of the spices.

Finish the seasoning by adding red vinegar, whole chillies and lime juice. Serve this lovely dish with Zanzibar pancakes (*mikate ya maji*).

BOKO BOKO

Preparation time: 1 hour

Boko Boko is the name for a dish more commonly known by its Arabic name, *harisah*, originally from Morocco and Algeria. It is a sort of heavy porridge prepared from shredded meat, bulgur wheat or cracked wheat (as used in couscous), and spices. The dish was brought by Arab settlers many hundred of years ago. The name *harisah* should not be confused with harissa sauces or paste.

Between 1856 and 1859, Richard Francis Burton travelled from Zanzibar to Lake Tanganyika, to and fro, and he was given *Boko Boko* every day until he named the dish 'the roast beef of East Africa'.

i) First recipe

INGREDIENTS

1kg mutton with bones	3 cups or 700g bulgur wheat or
2 cinnamon sticks	cracked wheat
1 tsp cumin powder	5 spoons kismayuu ghee
1 tsp turmeric powder	1 tsp grounded black pepper
	4 cups water

METHOD

In a large bowl, rinse the wheat until clean. Cover it with water and let it soak overnight. Drain it before cooking.

Place the meat in an iron pot. Add 4 cups of water and spices. Cover and bring to boil. Cook for 20 minutes.

Remove meat, but not the broth from the cooking pot and set aside. Skim any froth from the broth and throw it away. Stir wheat into the pot and cover. Reduce heat to simmer.

As the wheat begins to cook, remove meat from the bones. Shred it and return it to the pot. Stir until the meat and wheat are well mixed. Cover tightly and continue to cook for two hours on a very low heat. Check occasionally and add water if necessary.

When wheat is tender and fully cooked, add the ghee and stir it forcefully to turn it into a heavy but smooth porridge.

Serve the *Boko Boko* with sweet sour lime sauce, melted butter and sugar syrup.

ii) Second recipe

Preparation time: 1 hour

INGREDIENTS

½kg lamb	*1½ tsp liquid tail*
l water	*¼ tsp cumin*
½ stick cinnamon	*½ tsp cinnamon*
¾ tsp salt	*½ tsp lemon juice*
5 ounces of cracked wheat	*1kg tail*
1dl milk	

METHOD

The meat is boiled, then wheat is put on it until it gives up its starch. Then the meat is plucked off the bones and pounded and returned to the porridge. Some add milk.

Cut the lamb into a few large pieces (say the size of lamb chops), put in the water, add stick cinnamon and salt. Bring to a boil. Add the cracked wheat. Cook about ½ hour.

Remove the lamb (that is why it is in only a few pieces). Cut the lamb up, pound in a mortar almost to a paste, then put it back in. Add milk. Cook for another hour at a low temperature.

Render out tail liquid, sprinkle it, cumin, cinnamon, and lemon over the *Boko Boko* when you serve it.

NDIZI NA UTUMBO (BANANAS WITH CALF INTESTINES)

Preparation time: 1½ hour

Ndizi is the Swahili word for bananas and *utumbo* is the Swahili word for intestines. This recipe can be either *Ndovi na urumbo* (bananas with calf intestines) or *Ndizi na utumbo*. The following recipe is typically Comoran; these islands have played a very big role in colouring the culinary culture in Zanzibar. You can prepare the dish with meat and you will have also a good taste. I just prefer this recipe because of my historical background. I remember when I came to Zanzibar in 1985, I called my aunt, the late Bi Shifaa, and ordered this dish, not only because it was special, but it possesses a French culinary taste in the French tradition of '*les tripes de Marseilles*'.

INGREDIENTS

1 cup water	*1 cup coconut milk (canned is OK)*
¼kg towel intestines *and ¼kg*	*1 bay leaf (optional)*
string intestines.	*10 pce green hard bananas peeled*
1 tsp salt	*and bisected in the middle*
½ tsp black pepper	*1 spoon of oil*
1/2 onions, thinly sliced	*½ pce lime juice*
2 cloves fresh garlic	*2 whole chillies*

METHOD

Cut the towel intestines into bite-sized triangles of 5 cm each and the string intestines about one meter each, leave as it is.

Start to prepare the towel intestines pieces by fastening them to the string intestines pieces; tie them nicely so that they do not open very easily. In a pot or pan, bring five cups of water to a boil. Add the calf intestines, salt and pepper. Cover, reduce heat, and simmer.

While the intestines are simmering, heat oil in a separate pan. Fry the chopped onions and garlic for a few minutes. Add the bananas. Reduce heat. Add coconut milk and bay leaf. Cover and simmer.

Add the already cooked calf intestines in the middle of the bananas. Cook for 10 minutes or until the intestines are done and the bananas are tender.

Adjust seasoning by adding a little bit of lime juice to taste and two whole chillies.

COMORAN BEEF AND SPINACH STEW

Preparation time: 45 minutes

INGREDIENTS

6 small fresh tomatoes
1 fresh hot chilli, whole
4 medium onions, whole
¼ cup green bell pepper
6 tbs vegetable oil
1 lb stewing beef, cut in cubes
1 cup water (or beef broth)
¼ tsp sugar

¼ tsp salt
2 tsp cayenne (more or less to taste)
1½ tsp minced fresh ginger
1 lb fresh spinach
1 small tin tomato purée
1dl fresh tamarind juice
juice of half a lime
1dl red vinegar

METHOD

Combine the chilli, tomatoes, onions, and green bell pepper in a food processor, until the vegetables are minced but not puréed.

Heat the oil in a large, cast iron pot, and sauté the vegetables and beef for 5 minutes over high heat.

Add the tomato purée, water, sugar, salt, cayenne and ginger. Cover, lower the heat, and simmer for 2 hours. Stir occasionally to keep from burning.

Meanwhile, soak the spinach in warm water for 15 minutes. Then rinse thoroughly, separate, rinse again (and even a third time if you want to be extra careful), shred coarsely, and set aside.

After 2 hours, add the spinach to the pot and cook over medium heat for 30 minutes, until the water is gone and the spinach is cooked.

Finish the seasoning of the stew by adding tamarind juice, lime and vinegar

About half an hour before serving, prepare the coconut rice. Serve the stew with coconut rice.[*]

Opposite: Hamamni Baths, Mkonazini © Sultan Govani
Overleaf: Tembo Hotel, Zanzibar © Suleiman Abubakar

ZANZIBAR COFFEE GLAZED CHICKEN

Preparation time: 45 minutes

When you hear about this chicken then you will think the chef is crazy, or now this is too much; but it is *unguja*, a tropical dish which you will never forget after tasting it.

I prepared this dish, together with Forodhani Hotel and Restaurant Management College students from Dar es Salaam, when I visited Kizimbani Spice Gardens in 1999.

INGREDIENTS

$^1/_3$ cup packed dark brown sugar
2 tbs hot spicy ketchup
1 lime
1 tbs butter
2 tsp finely chopped ginger
1 tsp Tanzanian Nescafé 100%
Pure Instant Coffee Granules
$^1/_8$ tsp ground allspice (masala powder)

5 pce (about 1kg total) boneless, skinless chicken breast halves
2 large cloves garlic
1 tsp olive oil
$^1/_2$ tsp salt
$^1/_8$ tsp Zanzibar fresh ground green pepper granules
1 fresh Kizimbani orange[2]

METHOD

Combine the sugar, ketchup, fresh orange juice, lime juice, butter, ginger, coffee granules and allspice in a small saucepan. Bring to a gentle boil; stir until coffee and sugar are dissolved. Remove from heat; set aside.

Trim the chicken of any visible fat. With a sharp knife, make two diagonal slits about ½" deep on the top side of each breast.

Combine the garlic, oil, salt and pepper. Rub the mixture all over the chicken. Arrange slit side up on a rack in a shallow

---

[2] These oranges are very special; I think my uncle, Salim Himidi, will remember how tasty they are. I recall when I visited Kizimbani in 1999, the first thing I asked for was an orange to taste, and they still taste as good as they used to.

baking pan. Brush chicken with glaze; reserve remaining glaze. Refrigerate for 30 minutes.

Preheat broiler.

Broil the chicken for 5 minutes. Turn the chicken over; coat with reserved glaze. Broil for an additional 4 to 5 minutes. Turn chicken over again; coat with glaze. Broil for an additional 2 minutes or until the tops are sizzling and brown.

Serve the dish with Réunion Creole rice.

BANANA STEW WITH CHICKEN

Preparation time: 45 minutes

INGREDIENTS

4kg chicken thighs and legs
¼ cup fresh lemon juice
salt, fresh green pepper granules
3 tsp oil
1 medium onion, chopped
6 plum tomatoes, seeded, chopped
pinch of sugar

1dl dry red wine vinegar
½ cup low-sodium chicken broth
3 tsp butter
6 firm, ripe bananas, halved
lengthwise
½ cup grated creamy cheese

METHOD

Rinse the chicken and pat dry with paper towels. Rub it all over with lemon juice and sprinkle well with salt and pepper. In a deep, heavy-bottomed skillet or casserole with a lid, heat the oil over a medium heat. Brown chicken on all sides until golden brown. Remove from the skillet and keep warm. Add the onion, tomatoes and sugar to the pan and cook, stirring, until soft. Return chicken pieces to pan, add the red wine vinegar and broth, and bring to a simmer. Lower heat and cover pan. Simmer until chicken is tender, about 45 minutes. Set aside and keep warm.

In another large skillet, heat butter and sauté banana halves on both sides until golden brown. Arrange bananas on top of the chicken in the skillet and sprinkle them with the creamy cheese. Turn heat on low, cover and cook just until cheese melts. Use a large spatula to transfer the chicken with banana on top to plates.

GOAT MEAT CURRY STEW (*MCHUZI WA NYAMA YA MBUZI*)

Preparation time: 1 hour

INGREDIENTS

2kg lean goat meat (shoulder)	*1 tbs crushed green ginger*
oil for frying	*4 cloves garlic (crushed)*
1 sliced onion	*3 desert spoons curry powder*
3 tsp cumin seeds	*1 tbs paprika*
1½ tsp fenugreek seeds	*½ tsp chilli powder*
3cm piece cinnamon	*500g tomatoes*
8 whole cloves	*1 tsp cardamom*

METHOD

Cut meat into small pieces. Pour enough oil into a pan to cover the base and heat well. Add the sliced onion and cook until half browned. Add the cumin, fenugreek, cinnamon and cloves.

Cook gently until the onions are browned. Add ginger and crushed garlic, fry for 30 seconds. Add meat and cook until well browned.

Reduce heat and cook gently for 10 minutes. Add curry powder, paprika and chilli powder. Add peeled, chopped tomatoes and stir well to combine with other ingredients.

Place in an ovenproof dish. Stir in 500 ml water and sprinkle cardamom over the top.

Cover and simmer for 1½ to 2 hours. Add more water if necessary during cooking time. Serve with boiled jasmine rice and mango chutney.

Opposite: Zanzibar beauty © Sultan Govani
Overleaf: House of Wonders (back view) © Sultan Govani

CITRUS GOAT MEAT STEW

Preparation time: 20 minutes

INGREDIENTS

8 kid butterfly chops
125 ml lemon juice
2 tsp curry powder
2 tsp brown sugar

2 tsp butter
1 tbs cornflour
1 chicken stock cube, crumbled

METHOD

Marinate chops in a combination of lemon juice, curry powder and brown sugar for at least 10 minutes. Drain and reserve marinade.

Heat butter in a frying pan. Fry chops for 4 to 5 minutes on each side. Remove from pan and keep warm.

Blend cornflour with mango juice and add to pan with reserved marinade and crumbled stock cube. Bring to the boil, stirring constantly until thickened.

Add mango slices and allow to heat through. Serve chops with mango chutney accompanied by steamed basmati or jasmine rice.

FREE RANGE YOUNG GOAT WITH MANGO FRUIT AND ROASTED ROOT VEGETABLES

Preparation time: 1 hour

INGREDIENTS: GOAT

600g boneless young goat meat or fillet
*100g dried mung beans (*Choroko*)*

*100g half ripe Pemba mangoes (*Boribo*)*
salt and pepper

INGREDIENTS: ROASTED VEGETABLES

4 carrots
4 white Zanzibar parsnips
*(*mizizi ya figili*)*
50g Mtwara cashew nuts

100g dried cassava cut into triangle pieces.

INGREDIENTS: MANGO VINAIGRETTE

2 tbs red wine vinegar
1 tsp Zanzibar fresh ginger, finely shred
½ tbs olive oil

METHOD

Boil the mung beans in lightly salted water until soft, approximately 30 minutes.

Boil the dried cassava in a slightly salted water until it is soft.

Scrub the parsnips and carrots clean; trim and peel if necessary. Place them whole with cashew nuts in a greased ovenproof dish. Roast them for approximately 45 minutes at 175°C. Season with salt and pepper.

Mix the ingredients for the vinaigrette. Turn the hot roasted vegetables, mung beans and boiled cassava into the vinaigrette.

Cut a hole in the middle of the goat meat with a long, thin, sharp knife, and stuff it with half ripe mangoes. Sear the meat with butter and roast in the oven at 100°C for about 45 minutes.

Allow the meat to cool for 15 minutes before slicing and serving. Reduce the veal stock to 400 ml and add salt and pepper to taste.

Arrange the sliced goat meat on the roasted vegetables and mung beans. Spoon over the mango vinaigrette. Serve with spicy pilau rice.

SWEET AND SOUR GOAT MEAT CASSEROLE

Preparation time: 1 hour

INGREDIENTS: CASSEROLE

1.2kg prime goat meat　　　　　*8 Zanzibar peppercorns*
2 bay leaves　　　　　　　　　　*1 tbs salt*

INGREDIENTS: VEGETABLES

8 new carrots　　　　　　　　　*8 Tanga red onions*
1 Mtwara cassava　　　　　　　*1 pce Zanzibar figili salad*

INGREDIENTS: SWEET AND SOUR SAUCE

100 ml water　　　　　　　　　　*2dl fresh Greek yoghurt (*mtindi*)*
3 tbs white vinegar　　　　　　　*corn starch*
1 tbs brown sugar　　　　　　　*3 tbs fresh coriander, finely chopped*
25 g fresh basil leaves　　　　　*3 tbs parsley, finely chopped*
stock from the boiled meat　　　*salt and Zanzibar black pepper*

METHOD

Cut the mutton (goat meat) into chunks. Place in cold water, bring to the boil and skim thoroughly. Season and let the meat simmer for about 1 hour, until tender. Take the meat out.

Wash and cut the vegetables and simmer in the stock until ready. Take out and chill in ice cold water. Strain the stock and put aside.

Boil the water, vinegar, sugar and coriander stalks without a lid for about 20 minutes. Reduce the stock from the boiled meat to 400 ml. Add yoghurt and simmer until it thickens slightly, by using a little corn starch mixed with water as a thickener. Add the reduced vinegar stock to taste.

Heat the pieces of meat and the vegetables in the sauce. Stir in the herbs and add salt and pepper to taste. Serve the dish with Creole ghee rice.

GAWANI COCONUT COCK STEW

Preparation time: 1½ hour

This chicken stew is a tribute to Babu wa Gawani of Pemba Island, where we visited him every Sunday when we were children, together with my uncle the late Sk Said Ilyas. I am sure Mr Salim Himid, Mr Ali Himid and Ilyas will remember those Sundays when we would spend our day with the family of Babu wa Gawani. We always arrived at 10 a.m. As soon as we arrived we would take a walk through his farm which was full of cloves and fruit trees of every kind. But at exactly 1 p.m., we would be called to pray, and then served the following dish, together with coconut rice.

INGREDIENTS

*2 stalks fresh lemon grass (*mchai chai*)*
2 fresh hot chilly peppers, coarsely chopped
1 tbs coarsely chopped garlic (about 6 medium cloves)
1kg countryside cock, skinless, trimmed of fat and cut into 1" cubes
2 tsp Saleh Madawa curry powder
1 tsp finely grated, fresh peeled ginger (about ¹/₃" piece)
½ tsp brown sugar

¼ tsp freshly ground Zanzibar black pepper
1 tsp ghee
1 tsp home-made curry paste
1 tbs ghee, 1 cup coarsely chopped onions (about 2 medium onions), 1 cup canned chicken broth, ¹/₃ cup fresh or canned unsweetened coconut milk,
4 new potatoes in cubes

METHOD

Peel and discard the outer leaves of the lemon grass. With a sharp knife, cut off and discard the upper half of the stalks at the point where the leaves branch out. Thinly slice the remaining stalks.

Process the lemon grass, chilli peppers and garlic in a food processor until finely ground. Transfer the mixture to a mixing bowl. Add the chicken and the remaining marinade ingredients, mixing together until thoroughly blended. Cover and refrigerate for 30 minutes.

When ready, fry in a large skillet over high heat. Add the 1 tablespoon of ghee and heat until smoking hot. Add onions and stir-fry until golden brown, about 2 minutes.

Add the marinated cock and stir-fry until the chicken is golden on the outside and just cooked through on the inside, about 5 minutes. Add the broth, coconut milk, and potatoes. Continue to cook for 15 minutes longer, then remove from the heat. Transfer the stew to a warm bowl and serve immediately.

Opposite: Benn Haidari

Overleaf: Swahili roast beef prepared in Hotel St Jacque (Paris) East African Gastronomy Fair, 1994 © Benn Haidari

SWAHILI ROAST BEEF

Preparation time: 45 minutes

This is a delicious spicy roast beef, which I prepared in the Hôtel Softel St Jacques in Paris, where I attended the East African Gastronomy Fair in 1994.

INGREDIENTS

4 cloves garlic (minced)
1 tsp minced fresh ginger
2–3kg piece of steak
2dl fresh lime juice
3dl red vinegar
50g peeled almonds
5–4 spoons oil

1kg fine red onions, sliced
½ tsp cardamom
½ tsp ground black pepper
3 pce whole cinnamon
1 spoon pilau masala powder
½ tsp cumin
1 spoon salt

METHOD

Clean the steak by removing all the white fat from the top.

Warm up the frying pan with the oil. Fry the steak until it is golden brown in colour.

Take it out of the frying pan and spice it well. Place it on aluminium foil and put the rest of the spices on it together with the onions. Close it neatly.

Roast the steak in the oven for only 20 minutes at 250 to 360°C.

Take it out, leave it to cool in the foil paper until when you want to serve it cold. Slice it carefully and serve it with *kachumbar* or salsa.

Fish and Seafood

BLACK DORADO *CHUKU CHUKU*

Preparation time: 15 minutes

Living near the sea is just like living in paradise. Not only do you get fresh air from the sea, but also fresh fish. Fish is nice, preferably cooked and served whole. The best fish do not need a lot of fancy arrangement to do them justice. When I was working in the Hotel Amaranten in Stockholm, Sweden, I had a chef who really knew how to prepare fish, and hence I have come to know more about fish and how to prepare it. When I came to live in Mtwara, cooking fish was not new to me.

There are two kinds of dorado – in Swahili called *changu*. One is black, which means it possesses black scales, and the other is pink, meaning it has pink scales. The *changu* fish is a bony one. Although there are two main kinds of dorado, there are so many other sorts of these dorado. This kind of fish is found in the Indian Ocean coral reefs and coastal waters of Tanzania. They are about 100 cm long, maximum, and fished by using either seines, gill nets, hand lines, traps or bottom trawls.

INGREDIENTS

½l fish stock	*2 chopped garlic cloves*
1 fresh whole fish	*1 fresh chilli*
2 chopped whole tomatoes	*1dl heavy coconut cream*
3 sliced red onions	*1 chopped fresh ginger*
1dl fresh lime juice	*salt and pepper*

METHOD

Put the fish in the cold stock. Let it come to the boil and boil for a few minutes. Add the seasoning and let the dish boil for 10 minutes. Add the tomatoes, onions and leave it to simmer for about 5 minutes. Finish the cooking off with heavy coconut cream.

PAN-FRIED SESAME PATTED KINGFISH WITH BANANA CAKES, SERVED WITH TAMARIND SAUCE

Preparation time: 15 minutes

I do not know why this fish is called kingfish; if there is any meaning to the word then it really deserves the name, because it is the best fish I have eaten. It tastes better than salmon. If I had the telephone number of one of my chefs in Stockholm, Mr Tore Wretman, I would tell him to come here and taste this fish.

There are two types of kingfish available in Tanzania. One is *Cybium commersoni*; in Swahili, we call it *Nguru-maskati*. It is about 90 cm to 220 cm long. It has vertical dark bars (the juvenile is spotted). The fish is found between 15 and 200 m deep. They can be fished by drift gill nets and trawling.

The second one is called *Scomberomorus leopardus*; in Swahili, we call it *Nguru-kanadi*. It is between 80 cm and 120 cm long. You can catch it in coastal waters using gill nets, trawling and hand lines. The fish has elongated spots on its flanks.

INGREDIENTS: KINGFISH

300g kingfish	*1 egg*
300g margarine	*salt, pepper*
100g sesame seeds	

INGREDIENTS: BANANA CAKES

2 green bananas	*salt, pepper, and fresh crushed*
1 medium-sized red onion, chopped	*ginger*
1 clove garlic, crushed	*2 spoons sunflower oil*
1 raw potato	

INGREDIENTS: TAMARIND SAUCE

1 fresh bunch of brown tamarind	*1dl fresh cream*
½ bottle water	*4dl fish stock*
2 spoons vinegar	*salt, pepper*
3 spoons brown sugar	*2 tbs butter*
1dl fish stock	

METHOD

Gut the kingfish and fillet it. Remove all the bones from both fillets and cut them into a butterfly shape. Mix the raw egg with one spoon full of water and turn the butterfly kingfisher in the egg mixture and then on the sesame seeds. Preheat the frying pan, and melt the margarine accordingly. Fry the fish on both sides for about 4 minutes on each side until golden brown colour.

Grate the raw bananas after peeling, and peel the onions, garlic, potato and ginger. Mix together, and season the mixture. Form the cakes and pan-fry with sunflower oil in medium heat until they are golden brown in colour.

Put the bunch of tamarind in the blender together with water, and get the juice of tamarind strained.

Heat your saucepan, and brown the sugar in a very light colour. Flame the sugar with vinegar. Add the tamarind juice and the fish stock. Reduce the sauce until half liquid, season it and finish the cooking by adding cream and butter.

Put your tamarind sauce on a Chinese porcelain heater, and on top of the sauce put the fried butterfly kingfish and the banana cakes. Garnish the plate with parsley leaves.

JUMBO PRAWNS STEWED IN COCONUT CREAM

Preparation time: 15 minutes

Prawns are tasty when they are fresh. In Mtwara I was fortunate to live near the Indian Ocean. I got to know that when I didn't see many boats passing, next morning I wouldn't get any prawns, and so I would have to find another dish for the next day's lunch. Most of the prawns which came in to Mtwara town were fished either in Mozambique or in Lindi, but they were first class prawns.

INGREDIENTS

1kg prawns
1dl olive oil
1dl white wine
1dl fish stock
1dl heavy coconut cream
3 pce red onion
2 chopped tomatoes

1 crushed clove of garlic
salt, pepper, curry powder,
gurkmej *(in Swahili,* manjano*)*
½dl lime juice
1 tbs red vinegar

METHOD

Heat the saucepan and put in your olive oil. Sauté the prawns and the onions together. Add the crushed garlic, chopped tomatoes and the rest of spices. Add the wine and leave it to cook for a while, add the fish stock, and simmer the dish. Finish the stew with the heavy coconut cream and seasoning and leave it to cook for 5 minutes before you add the lime juice.

Serve it in your clay pot with coconut rice and garnish it with coriander.

Opposite: Changu fish (for Chuku dish) © U.S. Geological Survey
Overleaf: Shark and his fisherman at Funguni fishing harbour (for Chateaubriand)
  © U.S. Geological Survey

KINGFISH CHATEAUBRIAND ON A BED OF FRESH SPINACH WITH GRAPEFRUIT SAUCE

Preparation time: 25 minutes

Surprisingly, a kingfish fillet looks like a fillet of beef; the difference is only the colour. Fish fillet is white, while beef fillet is red in colour. These are some of experiments I did in Mtwara.

When I came to Zanzibar, I became loath to use products that had been flown halfway round the world, when Tanzania has quality ingredients near at hand. The New Zanzibar Cuisine is not about longing, it is the joy of living in a spice island like Zanzibar that is not so deeply affected by the seasons. Take grapefruit, for example: any time you need it, you just have to go to the market and you will find one, any time of the year.

INGREDIENTS: KINGFISH CHATEAUBRIAND

250g fillet of kingfish	*salt, pepper*
150g butter	

INGREDIENTS: KINGFISH ROE

1 whole kingfish roe	*1 red onion*
½l fish stock	*salt, pepper, bay leaf*

INGREDIENTS: FRESH SPINACH

1 bunch fresh spinach	*1 chopped red onion*
½dl fresh cream	*1 tbs margarine*
salt, pepper, fresh kizimbani	
grated nutmeg.	

INGREDIENTS: GRAPEFRUIT SAUCE

½l fish stock	*2 tbs butter*
4dl fresh grapefruit juice	*1 tsp maize flour.*
1dl white wine	*salt, pepper, sugar*

METHOD

After cutting the piece of fillet as needed, spice it, heat the frying pan and put the butter on the pan. Be careful that you do not burn the butter. Fry the kingfish piece for about 5 minutes each side, then finish cooking it in the oven.

Heat the saucepan, and put in a little bit of margarine. When the margarine melts, add the chopped onions and then the spinach. Mix and then add your cream. Season the spinach.

Put the fish stock in the saucepan and leave to boil. Add the white wine, and reduce to half of the liquid. Add the grapefruit juice and simmer the sauce while seasoning it gradually and tasting at the same time. Mix 1 teaspoon of maize flour with the remaining juice and thicken the sauce. Finish the preparation of sauce by adding the cream and butter, gradually.

Boil the fish roe in the fish stock, until ready.

Arrange the spinach in the middle of the serving plate, put the kingfish on the top of spinach and then slice the fish roe and garnish it on the top of the fish. Put the grapefruit sauce round the spinach. Serve the dish with dill potatoes.

GRILLED TUNA FISH

Preparation time: 15 minutes

The Indian Ocean is the sea of tuna fish. You can find all sizes of
tuna, from 2kg to 40kg, depending on how professional you are.
But this time it was not me who went to fish. It was in the days of
Ramadhan as I came from the Masjid Jawf mosque and passed the
Darajani market. I was astonished to see a lorry full of small tuna
fish. The price was ridiculous – I could not believe it. They cost
50 US cents for two pieces. I thought I was dreaming. I bought
four and went home. The following recipe was the exceptional
result.

INGREDIENTS

300g fresh tuna steaks, cut 1" thick
⅓ cup dry white wine
1 tbs Zanzibar fresh lime juice
1 tbs ghee
1 clove garlic, minced

2 tsp snipped fresh rosemary
1 tsp snipped fresh oregano
¼ tsp salt
4 lemon slices (optional)

MARINATING METHOD

Combine the wine, lemon juice, oil, garlic, rosemary, oregano,
and salt. Place fish in plastic bag set into a shallow dish. Add
marinade; seal bag. Turn fish to coat well. Chill for at least 1 hour
or up to 2 hours, turning fish once.

GRILLING METHOD

Discard marinade. Grill fish steaks on the greased rack of an
uncovered grill directly over medium coals for 5 to 8 minutes or
just until fish begins to flake easily when tested with a fork,
turning once.

To grill by indirect heat: Arrange preheated coals around a
drip pan in a covered grill. Test for medium heat above pan. Place
fish on the greased grill rack over drip pan. Cover and grill for 5

to 8 minutes, or just until fish begins to flake easily when tested with a fork, turning once.

Serve the tuna fish with coal-grilled cassava and mango chutney.

Opposite: Darajani market © Sultan Govani
Overleaf: Fish of Zanzibar Sea © U.S. Geological Survey

CREOLE SEAFOOD STEW

If the French are proud of their bouillabaisse then let me be proud of the fresh seafood dish that I named because of its origin. Wherever you go in the Indian Ocean, you will of course enjoy seafood. Zanzibar Island is the magnificent place to enjoy this dish. It was a holiday, which we call *Siku Kuu* or *Idd ul Fitr*, when I banished my wife from the kitchen and took the lead. What a day! The outcome is what you are about to read in this recipe.

I went to the fish market and came home with all the crustaceans and molluscs I needed. The rest is as follows.

INGREDIENTS: LOBSTER STOCK

8 dried lobster shells
3 red onions
1 bunch dill
1dl white wine
1l fish stock

1 tot cognac or brandy
1 tin concentrated tomato sauce
4 pcs bay leaves
black pepper granules

INGREDIENTS: SEAFOOD STEW

1 lobster, 500g
5 jumbo prawns
4 sea snails
3 abalones
4 small squids
3 tails of octopus
6 mussels
250g tuna fish fillet
3 red onions
3 cloves crushed garlic
1l heavy coconut cream

1 crushed fresh ginger
2 pce cloves
2 tbs Swahili curry powder
1 tbs red vinegar
1dl fresh lime juice
3 pce whole chillies
1 pce cardamom granules
1 pce whole cinnamon.
1dl white wine
1dl Cognac or brandy
1dl olive oil

METHOD

Grate the lobster shells thoroughly well by pounding them. Heat the stockpot and put the margarine in. Begin to sauté the shells while adding the vegetables. Flambé the products and mix together. Add the white wine, the fish stock. Boil for 30 minutes and no longer. Strain and reduce.

Clean all the seafood of sand and dry it well with a white cloth. If it is possible, take the shellfish out of their shells.

Heat your saucepan and add olive oil. Start with the lobster and then the onions. Flambé the lobster with cognac and then start adding the rest of vegetables while seasoning. Add the white wine, the vinegar and the lime, and reduce the stew until half liquid. Finish the stew by adding the heavy coconut cream and allowing it to simmer very slowly for about 10 minutes. Garnish the stew by adding fresh chopped coriander.

Opposite: Fishing dhow on a trip © Sultan Govani
Overleaf: Zanzibar fresh green peppercorns © Sultan Govani

Grilled Zanzibar Queen Prawns

Preparation time: 35 minutes

INGREDIENTS

½ tsp fresh lime zest
¼–½ tsp cumin
½ tsp oregano
½–1 tsp salt
½ tsp Zanzibar fresh green
peppercorns

2 tbs olive oil
3 tbs lime juice
3 fresh cloves garlic (mashed)
1kg shelled, uncooked Zanzibar
queen prawns

METHOD

Mix all those ingredients together and marinate the queen prawns.

Leave the prawns in the refrigerator until you start grilling.

THE ART OF GRILLING

The charcoal should not be too hot when you start grilling.

The best grill is a gas grill which uses lava stones, because you can regulate the heat.

When you start grilling, very slowly the shells of the prawns will start changing their colour, and then you can increase the temperature of the grill.

In the process of grilling, remember to brush the prawns with the marinade.

BARBECUED ZANZIBAR LOBSTERS

Preparation time: 25 minutes

INGREDIENTS

4 each Maine lobsters (500g each)
2 oz Worcestershire sauce
2 oz soy sauce
½ pound margarine or butter
2 each lemons, seeds removed
2 tbs ketchup

½ tbs fresh parsley
2 cloves garlic
½ tsp fresh oregano
1 tbs cracked Zanzibar fresh green
pepper granules
1 spoon fresh tamarind paste

METHOD

Mix all the ingredients and set aside.

Kill the lobsters by putting only the head of lobster in the hot boiling water for 5 minutes. Make sure the lobster is no longer alive before working on it.

Bisect each lobster into two pieces and marinate it with the marinade. Cool the lobsters in the refrigerator while you are preparing the coal grill.

On a hot grill, cook the lobsters until red in colour (usually about 5 minutes per side). Use the remaining marinade by brushing on the lobsters while grilling slowly under low heat. Remove lobsters from grill and serve with the best salsa you have and coconut rice.

Sweets And Desserts

Kashata

Preparation time: 45 minutes

Something between candy and a cookie, Eastern Africa's *Kashata* are a popular snack of Swahili origin. *Kashata* are usually made with peanuts or grated coconut, or both. They are cooked on the stove or over a fire, not in an oven like European biscuits or American cookies.

INGREDIENTS

2 cups sugar
2 cups fresh or moist grated coconut
(or two cups of dried grated coconut
moistened with a few tablespoons of
milk or water)... or 2 cups of
roasted peanuts, shells and skins
removed, briefly heated in a lightly
oiled skillet... or a mixture of both
coconut and peanuts
½ tsp ground cinnamon or
cardamom
a pinch of salt
½ cup wheat flour (optional)

METHOD

In a hot skillet, heat the sugar until it melts and just begins to brown.

Reduce heat and quickly add all other ingredients, stirring well as each ingredient is added. When all ingredients have been added to the mixture, continue stirring for about a minute, making sure everything is well mixed.

Scoop the mixture into a pan that has been lightly greased or lined with waxed paper. Let rest for a few minutes. Cut into squares or diamonds while still warm. Allow to cool and serve.

GROUNDNUT RUSKS

Preparation time: 50 minutes

INGREDIENTS

100g butter
85g sugar
2 eggs
210g flour

1 tsp baking powder
1 cup chopped fresh unblanched
groundnuts (peanuts)

METHOD

Cream the butter and sugar until fluffy, and the eggs one by one. Blend well so the mixture doesn't curdle.

Add the flour mixed with the baking powder and the ground-nut.

Place the mixture on a baking tray with greaseproof paper, three lengths of 30 cm each. Bake for about 10 minutes at 225°C.

Cut the lengths first in halves, then diagonally in pieces 1 cm wide. Separate them and dry them for about 30 minutes at 100°C.

Serve them with Zanzibar coffee spiced with ginger.

CASHEW NUT CAKE

i) First recipe

My stay in Mtwara gave me a lot of time to create new dishes, especially in the month of Ramadhan. Fortunately I fasted one time in the season of cashew nuts, and the following cake was one I prepared for my wife.

INGREDIENTS

100g butter
250g sugar
4 eggs

150g grounded cashew nuts
200g boiled cold pressed sweet potatoes.

METHOD

Mix the softened butter until white and fluffy.
  Add the egg yolks one at a time and mix thoroughly.
  Mix in the cashew nuts and the sweet potatoes.
  Beat the egg whites until stiff, fold them into the mixture with care (do not use whisk when mixing).
  Pour into a well greased and bread crumbed baking tin. Bake for about 50 minutes at 175°C.
  Let the cake rest for a while in its baking tin.

Serve the cake with lightly whipped cream after the *futari*.

ii) Second recipe

Preparation time: 1 hour

INGREDIENTS

2 litres full fat milk
¼ tsp cinnamon powder
½ cup (100g) sugar

40g margarine
250g cashew nuts, slivered
whipped cream

Pour the milk into a heavy-bottomed non-stick pan and bring to the boil.

Add the cinnamon and mix well. Simmer till the milk reduces to half, stirring continuously. Add the sugar and increase the flame stirring continuously, till the sugar has dissolved. The mixture may appear curdled, but continue to simmer and stir till it thickens. Keep stirring on a high flame till all the liquid evaporates. Add the margarine and mix well.

Meanwhile, grease a 200 mm (8") diameter cake tin and decorate the base with the slivered cashew nuts. Pour the hot milk cake mixture on it and cover with aluminium foil.

Cool to room temperature and then chill. Turn the cake over onto a serving plate.

Garnish with whipped cream and cashew nuts.

MOFA BREAD ROLLS

Preparation time: 24 hours

One of my lovely memories of Ramadhan in Zanzibar when I was a kid is when I was sent to Funguni by the late Syed Hassan Sheikh to buy *Mkate wa mofa* after coming back from the *darsa* (school)at the Masjid Jawf mosque. Whenever I gave the mofa bread to Syed Hassan I got a present, and of course it was *thumni* (half a shilling, or 50 cents at that time), which I would use when I went to Forodhani after Taraweikh. I always got one mofa loaf extra, which I hid in my white robe and ate at home.

The taste was very special, and extraordinary. Syed Hassan had diabetes and so his bread was mofa. I wish I had been old enough in those days to be able to ask the real recipe for how they did it; but better late than never. At last I checked everywhere, and when I got it I had to try it. For those who have diabetes, the following is the recipe for mofa.

INGREDIENTS

*800 ml or 3 cups sour milk (*mtindi*)*	*1 clove garlic, chopped*
1 onions, very finely chopped	*1kg Atta flour.*
(already sautéed)	*1 tbs salt*

METHOD

Dissolve the salt in the sour milk. Mix the rest of the ingredients and knead to a firm dough. Cover the dough with white cloth and leave in the dark place for the whole night.

Take out the dough next day and knead lightly and divide into two parts. Roll each part into a disc, and divide into twelve equal triangles. Roll the pieces towards the tip of the triangles to shape the rolls.

Leave on a baking tray for about 30 minutes while heating your oven to 225°C.

Bake for about 15 to 20 minutes. Serve the rolls hot or cold.

BENN'S FRUIT SALAD

Preparation time: 35 minutes

This recipe is a tribute to Pemba Island, the island of my child-hood, and the island which taught me how to depend on myself, by cooking my own food, when I was in primary school and Fidel Castro Secondary School. Pemba is a paradise of fresh fruits, and jungle spices.

You can get anything you want as far as fruits and vegetables are concerned. Spices – like ginger, green peppers, cloves – this is their home.

INGREDIENTS

3 fresh cloves	*breadfruit*
1 cup sugar	*cucumber (take out the seeds)*
2 cups water	*water melon (take out the seeds)*
pawpaw	*sweet bananas (small ones are*
pineapple	*preferable)*
mango	

METHOD

Boil the water and sugar together, until it is half of the liquid. In short it has to become light clove syrup. Take out the cloves and throw them away. Leave the light syrup to cool in the refrigerator.

Cut your fruits into small cubes and put them in the cold clove syrup. Leave the fruit salad to get cold enough before you serve it.

You can serve this fruit salad with vanilla ice cream or whipped cream on the top.

Opposite: Pressing sugar cane at Forodhani Gardens © Sultan Govani
Overleaf: Jack fruit on the tree © Sultan Govani

ZANZIBAR ROSE APPLE (*TUFAHA*) SERVED WITH LAPPACEUM (*SHOKISHOKI*) CREAM

Preparation time: 35 minutes

This is one of the best desserts I have ever tasted in my life as a cook. The taste is very tropical and I must say it competes with French cuisine. There is a story of an Englishman who was shown the tree on which this fruit grows. The fruit was high up in the tree, so the Englishman exclaimed, 'It's too far!' The Swahili guide who was showing him the fruit thougt the name was 'toofaa'; in Kiswahili the prefix for names is 'm'. So the fruit was called 'tufaah', and the tree named 'mtufaah'.

INGREDIENTS

12 red rose apples	*2 pieces of fresh cinnamon (not*
1 cup sugar	*powder)*
	3 cups of water

INGREDIENTS: LAPPACEUM CREAM

130g sugar	*6 egg yolks*
1 cup milk	*6 lappaceum*

METHOD

Take the seeds out of the rose apples and put aside.

In a big pot bring some water, fresh cinnamon and sugar to boil. Add the rose apples for 10 minutes. Take the pot and leave the rose apples to cool in the liquid you cooked, or put in the refrigerator.

Peel the fruit and take out the white lappaceum and mix with half a cup of milk in the mixer.

Mix the sugar with the rest of the milk, and fold in the egg yolks. Beat over moderate heat until the cream thickens.

Mix the hot cream with the lappaceum mixture, and stir until cold.

Leave in the refrigerator overnight, so it becomes thick and gorgeous.

Serve the cinnamon spiced rose apple with lappaceum cream the next day. What a wonderful taste you will experience!

Sweetmeat (Halwa) using Carrots

Preparation time: 35 minutes

INGREDIENTS

4 teacups grated carrots   *a pinch of cardamom powder*
8 tbs sugar   *5 tbs ghee*
5 tbs skim milk powder   *1 tbs arrowroot*
2 tsp almonds, sliced

METHOD

Cook the carrots in boiling water, then mash them.

Heat the ghee and add the mashed carrots and the arrowroot. Fry for 2 minutes.

Add the sugar and cook for 2 to 3 minutes. Then add the skim milk powder and cook for a few minutes, stirring continually. Sprinkle the cardamom while stirring.

Take it out and put on the plate. Add the peeled almonds on the top.

Serve it hot or cold with Zanzibar ginger coffee.

Comoran Laddu

Preparation time: 45 minutes

INGREDIENTS

¾ cup (100g) coarsely ground raw rice
¾ cup (100g) powdered sugar
⅓ cup (60g) ghee

¼ tsp cardamom powder
2 spoons coarsely grounded black pepper

METHOD

Mix together the sugar and pepper and keep aside.

Melt the ghee in an iron dish, add the rice and cook over a low flame stirring continuously until it is well cooked. Add the cardamom powder and mix well.

Remove from the heat and pour onto a plate. Cool completely.

Mix together the rice mixture and sugar.

Divide into 7 equal portions and shape into laddus.

Leave them to dry.

Sweet Dumplings (*Kaimati*)

Preparation time: 1 hour

One of the Ramadhan desserts I ate when I was a kid was Bii's sweet dumplings (Bii was Abdallah Abdulrahman Bomba's mother). She cooked the best dumplings and I really enjoyed them. This recipe is in actual fact hers; she used a little bit of fresh yoghurt (*mtindi*). The meaning of mixing yoghurt in the batter is to make the dumplings dry after frying.

INGREDIENTS

3 cups white flour
2 tsp yeast with a pinch of sugar
(mixed)

2/3 cup yoghurt
½ cup warm water
oil for frying

METHOD

Add to flour a little salt, water and the yoghurt, and mix to a thick batter. Leave aside for 6 hours.

Mix the yeast with the sugar and warm water; leave to ferment.

Add the yeast to the batter and mix until batter peaks; leave aside for a further three hours.

METHOD OF FRYING

Heat the oil. Shape the batter into little balls, and put them a few at a time in the hot deep oil and fry until golden brown.

Dumplings should be entirely covered with oil during frying. Take great care as the oil will splash during the course of frying.

When frying is complete, soak the dumplings in syrup and serve hot.

SYRUP (*SHIRA*)

INGREDIENTS

2 cups sugar   *1 tbs rose water*
1 cup water   *juice of half a lemon*

METHOD

Put the water in a pan with the sugar and place over a medium heat; bring to the boil and allow to boil for 10 minutes, removing the froth as it appears.

Add the lemon juice and leave to simmer for 10 minutes; finish with the rose water.

PINEAPPLE SWEET CHEESE SERVED WITH PAWPAW PURÉE

Preparation time: 15 minutes

INGREDIENTS

*1¼ cups curdled milk (*mtindi*)*   *1 ripe pawpaw*
¼ cup sugar   *½ tsp cinnamon powder*

METHOD

Add the sugar to the curdled milk and mix gently.

Cook on a very low flame in a dish stirring continuously with a flat wooden spoon.

Remove the dish from the flame at regular intervals so as not to overheat the sweet cheese. If it does overheat, it will become grainy and the fat will separate.

The sweet cheese is ready when it leaves the dish and is neither too dry not too moist. It should have the consistency of a very soft dough. Peel the pineapple and slice it 3 cm thick.

Fry the sliced pineapples and garnish the slices with the sweet cheese on the top.

METHOD: PAWPAW PURÉE

Peel the pawpaw and mix it in the blender with a little bit of sugar, if needed, and cinnamon powder.

Strain the purée.

Put the pineapple sweet cheese on the plate and garnish with pawpaw purée around.

Serve the dessert.

BAKED HALVA

Preparation time: 1 hour

Medium Syrup

INGREDIENTS

4 cups finely chopped cashew nuts
1 tsp ground cinnamon
½ tsp Saleh Madawa pilau spices
½ tsp Zanzibar fresh ground
nutmeg
¼ tsp Zanzibar ground cloves

¼ cup sugar
20 filo pastry sheets (sambusa
sheets)
1–½ cups unsalted butter, clarified,
or margarine, melted

METHOD

Prepare Medium Syrup. Set aside to cool. Preheat oven to 175°C.

Lightly butter a 13" x 9" baking oven pan. Set aside.

In a medium bowl, combine Mtwara cashew nuts, cinnamon, pilau spices, nutmeg, cloves and sugar. Set aside.

Stack filo pastry sheets on a flat surface. Trim to fit pan. Cover with plastic wrap to prevent drying out.

Layer 12 filo sheets in baking oven pan, brushing each sheet with clarified butter or melted margarine. Spread 1 cup nut mixture over layered filo sheets. Top with 4 more filo sheets, brushing each with butter or margarine.

Spread with 1 cup nut mixture. Layer 4 more filo sheets, brushing each with butter or margarine. Spread with remaining nut mixture. Top with 8 remaining filo sheets, brushing each with butter or margarine.

Brush top sheet with remaining butter or margarine. Cutting all the way through pastry, cut into 1" diamond shapes without removing from pan

Bake for 30 minutes, then reduce heat to 95°C and bake for 30 minutes or longer until golden brown.

Pour cooled syrup over warm pastry. Allow to stand for several hours before serving.

Syrup

INGREDIENTS

3 cups sugar   *2 tsp lemon juice*
1½ cups water

METHOD

Combine all the ingredients in a large, heavy saucepan.

Bring to the boil, stirring frequently. Reduce heat. Once mixture boils and sugar is dissolved, do not stir or syrup may cloud or crystallise.

Cook, uncovered, over medium-low heat until a candy thermometer registers 100 to 102°C. At this temperature, syrup dropped from a cold metal spoon will fall in a sheet.

Remove from heat. Cool.

Use immediately or refrigerate in a plastic container with lid.

Muesli Ice Cream

Preparation time: 25 minutes

Muesli is a breakfast cereal which comprises of cornflakes, rolled oats, nuts, raisins, spices and dried apples.

INGREDIENTS: ICE CREAM

2 cups milk	*¹/₃ cup powdered sugar*
1 cup milk powder	*1 tsp vanilla essence*
½ cup (100g) fresh cream	

INGREDIENTS: GRANOLA BARS

½ cup crushed cornflakes	*1 tbs melon seeds (*charmagaz*)*
½ cup quick rolled oats	*1 tbs raisins*
¼ cup mixed nuts (almonds,	*½ cup sugar*
pistachios, walnuts, cashew nuts),	*oil to grease*
chopped	

METHOD

Lightly roast the oats, nuts and melon seeds and keep aside to cool.

When cooled, mix together the cornflakes with the nuts, toasted oats, melon seeds and raisins. Add the sugar in a heavy-bottomed pan and melt it over a gentle heat, stirring continuously till the sugar is light brown in colour (caramelised).

Remove from the fire, add the rest of the ingredients and mix well. Pour this mixture onto a greased marble or stone surface.

Using a large greased rolling pin, roll it out lightly to form a square of approximately 200 mm x 200 mm (8" x 8").

While it is still warm, cut out rectangular bars of 25 mm x 100 mm (1" x 4").

For the ice cream, crush into small pieces and keep aside.

METHOD: ICE CREAM

Combine all the ingredients together and whisk well till the sugar dissolves.

Pour into a shallow container. Cover and freeze till it is semi-set.

Churn in a blender till all the ice crystals break down and transfer into a shallow container.

Add the crushed granola bars and mix lightly.

Transfer into a shallow container, cover and freeze till set. Scoop and serve.

LIME ZALBIYA

1 cup plain flour
1 tsp gram flour
½ tsp fresh yeast, crumbled

1 tbs melted ghee
1 tsp sugar
3 drops lemon yellow food colouring

INGREDIENTS: SYRUP

½ cup sugar
a few strands saffron

¼ tsp lime juice

OTHER INGREDIENTS

oil or ghee for deep frying

METHOD

Sieve the flour and gram flour together.

Dissolve the yeast in 1 tbs of water.

Mix the flour mixture, yeast solution, ghee, sugar and lemon yellow food colouring with 2/3 cup of water to make a thick batter, making sure no lumps remain.

Keep aside for 10 minutes.

METHOD: SYRUP

Dissolve the sugar with ½ cup of water and simmer for 5 minutes till the syrup is of 2 string consistency.

Add the saffron and lemon juice and mix.

Remove from the fire and keep aside.

DEEP-FRYING METHOD

Heat the ghee or oil in a broad saucepan (the oil should be approximately 25 mm or 1" deep).

Fill the zalbya batter into a piping bag with a single hole nozzle, or a thick cloth with a small hole in the centre which is finished with button-hole stitch.

Press out round whirls into the hot ghee working closely from outside to the centre of the whirl (approx. 50 mm or 2" diameter).

Deep-fry the zalbiya till golden brown and transfer into warm sugar syrup.

Drain immediately and serve hot.

BENN'S TROPICAL FRUIT CAKE

Preparation time: 1½ hour

INGREDIENTS

100g butter
250g sugar
4 eggs
150g dried tropical fruits (mangoes, pineapples, bananas, pawpaw) cut in small pieces.
250g boiled cold pressed potatoes.

METHOD

Mix the softened butter and sugar until white and fluffy. Add the egg yolks, one at a time, and mix thoroughly. Then mix in the dried fruits and potatoes.

Beat the egg whites until stiff, fold them into the mixture with care. Pour into a well greased and bread-crumbed baking tin, 20 to 22 cm in diameter.

Bake for about 50 minutes at 175°C. Let the cake rest for a while in the tin. It is important that it should be intact and handsome when it is turned out.

Chutneys

Mango Chutney (Kachumbar ya Embe)

i) First recipe

Preparation time: 50 minutes

INGREDIENTS

2 cups red onion, diced
½dl red vinegar
¾kg light brown sugar or honey
salt and pepper
2 pce tomatoes, diced

1 pce hot chilly, diced
1 tsp curry powder
1dl olive oil
2 pce ripe Pemba mangoes, diced

METHOD

Place red onion, vinegar and brown sugar in a stainless pot and bring to a simmer. Cook for about 30 minutes.

Add tomatoes, chillies and curry powder and cook for a further 20 minutes (or until syrupy).

Remove from heat and add the mango.

ii) Second recipe

Preparation time: 5 days

INGREDIENTS

½ cup chickpeas
1½ cups grated raw mango
1 tsp turmeric powder
1 tsp brown sugar
1 tbs curry powder
1 tbs fennel seeds
½ fresh crushed ginger
1 tsp mustard seeds
14 whole red chillies (whole

1 tbs chilli powder
1 ¼ cups Mtwara sesame oil
1 tbs salt

METHOD

Combine the grated mango, turmeric powder and salt and put aside for 30 minutes.

Squeeze out all the mango water using a muslin cloth and keep aside. Set the grated mango aside separately.

Soak the chickpeas and mustard seeds in the mango water overnight. Refrigerate the grated mango.

Combine the crushed ginger, fennel seeds, brown sugar, whole red chillies, chilli powder and soaked chickpeas mixture with the grated mango. Mix well.

Heat the mustard oil. Cool it and add to the prepared mixture.

Bottle the pickle in a sterilised glass jar.

The pickle is ready to eat after 3 to 4 days.

Store it in a cool place.

Opposite: Boats ready for fishing trip © Sultan Govani

Overleaf: On the way to search for fresh food (morning trip in the country side) © Sultan Govani

My Mango Pickles

Preparation time: 5 days

INGREDIENTS

*3 cups (375g) raw mangoes, cut
into 25 mm or 1" cubes
1 cup soaked chickpeas
1 cup (100g) dried mixed fruits
2 tsp cumin seeds
1 tsp coriander seeds
1 tsp turmeric powder*

*2 tsp fennel seeds crushed
½ tsp fresh crushed ginger
1 cup dried raisins
1 tbs chilli flakes
1 cups mustard oil
4 tbs salt*

METHOD

Place the mango pieces on a large sieve. Cover the sieve with a clean muslin cloth and place it under the sun for 4 to 6 hours.

Drain the chickpeas. Set aside.

Combine coriander seeds, raisins, dried fruits, turmeric powder, fennel seeds, chilli flakes, mustard oil and salt and mix well.

Add the mango pieces and chickpeas and stir well.

Bottle the pickle in a sterilised glass jar.

Press the ingredients in the jar using the back of a spoon so that all the pickle ingredients are immersed in oil.

Keep the jar in the sun for 4 to 5 days, stirring the ingredients in the jar occasionally. This pickle is then ready to serve.

TOMATO CHUTNEY

Preparation time: 1½ hour

INGREDIENTS

500g firm ripe tomatoes
1 ¾ cups (350g) brown sugar
¼ cup carrots, finely chopped
3 cloves garlic, peeled
10 to 12 Zanzibar fresh green peppercorns
3 dried Zanzibar cloves
1 fresh Zanzibar cardamom
12 mm. (½") piece Zanzibar fresh ginger, chopped

4 whole red chillies
1 tsp red vinegar
½ tsp coriander
1 tsp chilli powder
⅛ tsp fresh Zanzibar nutmeg powder
⅛ tsp curry powder
2 tbs almonds, peeled
½ tsp salt

METHOD

Blanch the tomatoes in boiling water. Peel the skin and cut each into 2 halves. Squeeze out the juice and seeds. Keep the tomato flesh and juice aside separately.

Strain the tomato juice; discard the seeds. Add the sugar to the tomato juice and leave aside for half an hour.

Chop the tomato flesh into large pieces.

In a pan, add the tomato juice and sugar mixture, tomato pieces, carrots, garlic, peppercorns, cloves, black cardamom, ginger and red chillies and cook over a very slow flame, stirring occasionally.

Cook for about 40 to 45 minutes until the mixture has reduced to less than half its original quantity and the syrup is a string consistency.

Remove from the heat and cool completely. Add the vinegar, coriander seeds, chilli powder, nutmeg, curry powder, almonds and salt and mix well.

Bottle in a sterilised glass jar and store refrigerated.

Index

11874230R0010

Made in the USA
Lexington, KY
07 November 2011